Leading America Back to Work

Reimagining Today's Workplace

Leading America Back to Work

Reimagining Today's Workplace

JASON GROBBEL
WITH DAN CALABRESE
FOREWORD BY HERMAN CAIN

Cover by Samantha Grobbel
Back cover photo by John F. Martin Photography

Copyright © 2018 by Jason Grobbel

All rights reserved.

I want to dedicate this book to my mother, Judge Beverly Curran.

Although I was 6th of 8 children, she and I had a special connection. Starting at a very young age, we would discuss and debate the various relationships within the families of our large Catholic neighborhood. She taught me that the family is a microcosm of the world. I learned about emotional intelligence and really caring about people with understanding. I learned about faith and spirituality. I learned that the greatest form of love is sacrificial love. She was a great woman and a great teacher.

Table of Contents

FOREWORD
By Herman Cain

When I talk about business people driving the change in this country, Jason Grobbel is just the type of leader I have in mind.

I had the opportunity to talk with Jason during Summer 2017 through our mutual colleague Dan Calabrese, and Jason told me in detail about the steps he had taken to strengthen the work force at Grobbel's. The change had been so dramatic, he explained, he felt he owed it to the rest of the business community to share his methods with them in a book.

What you're about to read is the realization of that vision, and I'm so glad he followed his inspiration and got it done.

I don't know if Americans by and large realize what an untapped resource the work force is, and how underutilized it's been in recent years. When the work force participation rate sunk to under 63 percent in the middle of the 2010s decade, many of us who have owned and run businesses understood why that had happened.

Part of it was that public policy incentives had discouraged work and too easily rewarded the avoidance of it. But much of it came from the fact that a new generation of workers was looking for different things than their parents and grandparents had wanted – and too many business owners didn't understand these priorities or know how to deliver on them.

That doesn't mean that employers should simply cater to the agendas of their employees all the time. That's not how it works and it never can work that way. But neither should it be a my-way-or-the-highway proposition with the employers dictating everything that happens.

What too few people understand – and honestly, I wish more employees understood this – is that an employment relationship is a mutual thing. Each party needs to get something out of it. The employee needs an income. Fine. We all understand that. The employer, on the other hand, needs productivity. That gives employees a lot more leverage in the employer/employee relationship than most of them realize they have. Those who seek to improve themselves and their performance are in a position to make themselves indispensable in the eyes of their employers. They don't just have to beg for wage increases, vacation time or whatever.

When you really produce, you can exercise a lot of say over the conditions of your employment. Why? Because if you look at the state of today's work force, you'll see that employers are dying to find people like that. The U3 unemployment rate – the one that doesn't count people who've dropped out of the work force – is just above 4.0 percent. That's basically full employment, which means that just about everyone who knows how to show up consistently and do a good job already has a job.

The only way you can fill a vacancy is to steal away a

worker from someone else by outbidding them or by luring someone who's left the workforce back into it. If you're one of those workers, that puts you in the driver's seat. If more workers understood this and did the things that allow them to reap the benefits of it, we'd all be better off.

And the companies that understand these dynamics are going to have a huge competitive advantage, because they'll be the ones attracting the work force of today and putting them in the best position to deliver on their potential. That's why I'm so impressed by what Grobbel's has done, and by Jason's determination to tell the world about it.

He didn't have to. He could have held this close to the vest and treated it like a trade secret. It probably would have served as a competitive advantage had he done so. But it was clear in talking to him that he saw the issue as much bigger than simply what would benefit his company's bottom line.

Jason understands that America's economic health is based on productivity, and that we can't be productive without workers who know how to produce, and want to, and are provided with a setting in which they can. It really is up to employers to make that happen, and we're in a better position now than ever before to do that.

We all owe Jason a debt of gratitude for setting forth in this book the way to get it done.

1

Where Have All the Workers Gone?
(And Why?)

The American workforce doesn't really work. It could. But right now, it doesn't.

And it's really not the fault of the workers. Some workers are better than others, of course, but for the most part people work within the system they have. You can only produce as much as the system permits you to produce, and even the best workers can't rise above the inherent limits of the system in which they operate.

We can make this better. This book is about how we do that. It's about how we change the fundamental assumptions that drive how the workplace functions in the American business sector. It's about how we give our employees a real opportunity to produce at the level that would result in real prosperity – for them, for us, and for the nation as a whole.

But first, we need to understand why this is a problem.

Several years ago, our company had an experience that really opened my eyes. Our workforce was humming along nicely, we thought, with the system we had implemented.

Cutting meat is a more intricate task than you might think, and we had a sizeable group of employees who had mastered our system. They were productive, efficient and reliable – and they needed to be, because this is an industry where you simply can't tell a customer that on a given day you don't have what they need.

Not even once. If you do, you're dead.

But we didn't think that would be a problem for us, until the day Immigration and Customs Enforcement (ICE) showed up to do a review of our workforce. We welcomed them, of course, because we operate legally, having collected all of the required I9 documentation on each and every employee and we had no reason to think we had any issues.

We were wrong.

It turned out that more than 50 of our employees – including some of those well-trained and highly productive people I mentioned above – presented false or forged documentation, and we could not continue employing them. Without getting into the legal minutiae, let's suffice it to say we had done nothing wrong and we were in no legal jeopardy. But we had no choice but to part ways with these people.

And it looked like a looming disaster for us. The amount of training these people had required to get to their level of proficiency took four to six months. And because of the demands of our industry, we didn't have four to six months to get new people up to speed. We didn't even have four to six weeks. Our customers would be gone. If we were going to survive, we had to completely rethink the way we trained our people, and what we trained them to do.

And this was not the fault of the employees who remained. They weren't dumb or incapable. But we had set up a system that couldn't be learned in the time we needed them to learn it. That was on us, not on them.

This is not to say a system is better just because someone can learn it quickly. But the more we looked at what we'd been doing, the more we realized it was only performing well in the context of long-time assumptions we'd made about how the workforce needed to operate. Necessity being the mother of invention, as they say, it was healthy for us to step back and question whether we were really operating in the best way we could.

And the more we looked at it, the more we realized we weren't. We were asking each employee to master a very complicated set of tasks. The complex nature of that assignment was actually limiting how productive each employee could be. Even though they did it well, it could only do so much for us.

So we completely rethought what we would ask employees to do. We broke down the process into several simpler steps and spread them across more people. Each person's assignment would be easier to learn and easier to master. And by designing a system that allowed each person's work to flow more simply into that of the next, we would be able to make the entire team more productive without anyone requiring months of training.

Yes, it was faster to learn, but that wasn't the be-all and end-all. The key was that our people were able to do more and do it better.

The more we studied what had happened, and how we had responded to it, the more we realized we had not put our people in the best position to succeed. Their assignments weren't in line with their needs, so their output wasn't a good match for their capacities or for our needs.

To put it a little more simply, we had assumed that existing systems were fine because they seemed to be fine. And we hadn't wanted to disrupt the status quo by thinking about new ways to do things – especially since there didn't seem to be any need for it. Only an existential crisis forced us to think about it differently, and our response to that crisis paved the way for a far better method of operating.

Both our company and our employees are better off today because we did this. I won't look back and say I'm glad we lost those people, because they were good people. But I'm glad the disruption forced us to challenge our own assumptions. We're stronger now.

I believe that in many ways, corporate America is in its own existential crisis. Not in the sense that we're a few steps away from disappearing. But our competitiveness is lagging. We're not producing anywhere near what we could, and should. We can't put that on our workers because for the most part we're not putting them in a position to succeed. Most of the assumptions about how the workplace should operate come from a time when people were different, incentives were different and technology was different.

Management is comfortable with existing systems because we've mastered the art of running them. The path of least resistance is to keep things the way they are. And if you're the person who advocates doing something different, you're taking a risk that might not work. Corporate America can be a pretty risk-averse place for that very reason. If you told everyone to change, and the change turns out to be a disaster, you might be history.

But the status quo can be a disaster too. It's just that it's a slowly simmering one you don't always recognize – until you step back and look at the big picture, and realize you're not doing as well as you should be.

So what do we do about it?

Everyone will tell you we need to train workers for the 21st century. That's true in the sense that training is obviously important. But it's not really the answer. We can't get ourselves out of the problem we're facing until we change the game, and start adapting jobs to people as they are today – not as they were 50 or 100 years ago.

That's not to say we can't learn anything from the innovations of the past. One of the most popular examples of this is also one of the best. It's the revolutionary way Henry Ford looked at the capacity of the workforce.

It seems impossible now, but in the late 19th and early 20th centuries, you had to pay as much as $10,000 for an automobile. That's about $275,000 in today's dollars. Why? Because they had to be handmade, individually, by master craftsmen. Only the wealthiest people could get them. But even if everyone suddenly became super-rich, that wouldn't have meant everyone could get a car. Because there weren't enough master craftsmen around to make them.

If cars were going to be accessible to the average person, then someone would have to come up with an entirely different way of producing them. It would have to be such a radical change that it would completely disrupt the established order.

That's what Ford did. He figured out a way to mass-produce automobiles such that he could sell them for $500 apiece. How could he do that? How could he reduce the cost of a product by 2,000 percent?

He did it by rethinking what would be expected of the workers building the car.

A master craftsman had to spend many years learning the craft he would perform. Every automobile maker in the world employed these master craftsman, and had to invest heavily over many years in their training.

What Henry Ford believed was that he could take "unskilled" workers and teach each of them one element of the master craftsman's job – not everything the master craftsman did, but just one part of it. And by putting enough of these workers in place on an assembly line, he could actually make his workforce 20 times more productive than the master craftsman.

Offering high wages, he lured farmhands from the south up to Detroit and assigned them straightforward roles they could be taught in a short amount of time. You often hear the story that he paid them these high wages so they could afford to buy the cars. His real motivation was not so altruistic, but it was just as brilliant. He needed the attractive wage to gather a large workforce, because the productivity of that large workforce would allow him to sell cars at very large volumes and make a healthy profit.

But before he could do that, he had to think differently than anyone had ever thought before about work and the people who would be doing it. He took into account their current situations, their level of skill and the role modern (at the time) technology could play in driving their productivity.

More importantly, he looked at the way things were being done at the time and was willing to question whether that was really the best way.

Ford encountered a lot of resistance to his ideas, precisely because they were disruptive. Industry didn't train workers to do what Ford wanted them to do. They didn't know how. They had never even thought of it. If Ford's ideas worked, everyone's ideas about work, people, training and productivity would have to change. That would cause problems for a lot of people.

But those who were willing to embrace the change would be able to grow and profit in ways their stuck-in-the-past counterparts would not.

And by the way, that scalability problem was solved. There could never be enough of the master-craftsman-built $10,000 cars for everyone, because there weren't enough master craftsmen to build them. But there were enough of the $500 cars, because the workforce that built those was 20 times as productive.

So the whole idea of the automobile and its role in American society had changed. It was no longer an exclusive product for the economic elite. Now everyone could aspire to own one. And that changed everything about how Americans lived, where they could live and where they could go.

It wasn't automation that made this happen. That played a role, but the key was specialization. That's what made it possible for each worker to become part of such a productive overall workforce.

I've always found it interesting that some people see that as demeaning to the worker. I've heard people ask, "Why would you want to just do one thing, all day, every day?"

To that, I ask this question: If you were on a pit crew of a NASCAR racing team, and your job was to change the left front tire every time that car came into the pit, would you consider that job demeaning? Almost no one would, because they would recognize how important the task was to the achievement of the larger mission.

An individual job on an assembly line is just as important. You're a specialist, and no one knows your particular role as well as you do. If you don't do it correctly, the whole system breaks down.

When people realize the importance of their role, they will have a better sense of their value, and their work will become more important to them. As it should.

Now, Henry Ford's disruptive vision for the workforce happened more than 100 years ago. It was based on his understanding of the people, the products and the technology of that time. We can learn from it – especially from his willingness to think differently – but the innovations we need today are different. Because today, everything is different. Technology. Culture. Economics. Lifestyles. Attitudes. Relationships. None of this is like it was 100 years ago, and that should come as no surprise to anyone.

And yet in so many ways, the way we think about work and workers really has not changed at all. We've gotten used to what worked well years ago, so we still do it that way. But the more we cling to the thinking of the past, the more it's costing us.

It's costing us in global competitiveness. It's costing us in retention. It's costing us in day-to-day performance. We're not doing as well as we could, and it's not because we don't want to. It's because it's been too long since we re-thought the way work is aligned with workers.

When we lost all those people following the ICE incident, we had to re-think some crucial assumptions we'd always made about our operational processes. That included the fundamental issue of how we trimmed our meat, and who would be qualified to do it.

Just consider the task of trimming briskets. With our old method, I had to find individuals who had the patience to work through a four-to-six-month development process before they could become truly effective at trimming briskets. We couldn't just go out and hire butchers because they're trained to trim an entire carcass, so when you limit them to just trimming a particular cut, you're not getting the same level of value out of them – and you're paying too much for what you do get.

By the way, you're paying people while you're training them, and you're also paying the trainers. So that four-to-six-month process had better yield you some excellent labor value on the other side.

But that's a moot point when you simply don't have that kind of time. In order to avoid falling into a potentially fatal period of non-productivity, we broke the process down into eight segments, and made a large-scale set of hires. Then we chose one segment for each new hire and trained them in less than two weeks to perform that segment.

The cost of the labor is a crucial issue. There is high-cost labor that produces high value, such that you can recoup your investment. But you can rarely scale it. It's extremely difficult to make a profit on high-cost labor in high volumes. It goes back to those $10,000 cars made by master craftsmen more than 100 years ago. You could sell some, but you couldn't sell them in mass quantities. Not enough people could afford to buy them. And even if they could, you couldn't find enough master craftsmen to make them in such quantities.

So here's the puzzle we're left with: How do you make work pay off for workers, and work with their lifestyles, without paying them more than you can earn back in the form of value?

Both sides of the equation, after all, are crucial. If you pay someone more than they can generate for you in value, you can't sustain that job. This is why you can't pay fast-food workers $15 an hour. Even the best workers can't generate enough value in the fast-food business model to make that a good investment. It has nothing to do with how hard they work or how much they need it. The nature of the product can't generate the return you need.

But trapping people in low-paying jobs with no path to better ones isn't the answer either. They may work hard to earn that wage while it's the only one they can access. But they won't push themselves to give you additional value because there will be no reward for doing so.

Why is it American business that needs to figure this out? Look at the state of the workforce and the answer becomes clear. Right now, we have nearly 40 percent of the work-capable population not even participating in the workforce. The latest statistics as I write this show that workforce participation is stuck at a mere 63 percent according to the Bureau of Labor Statistics. That remains close to its lowest point since 1978. Around the turn of the century it was nearly 68 percent, but it's been declining ever since.

As of early 2018, the number was improving somewhat, but it was still at a historically low point.

How do we account for that? A lot of people will be quick to talk about the work ethic of younger generations, or perhaps about too many public-sector incentives not to work. I'm not saying there's nothing to any of that, but as a general rule (and conceding that there are obviously some exceptions), people respond to the incentives of the marketplace. If 37 percent of American workers don't think it makes sense for them to even participate in the workforce, then what are they looking for that they don't think they're going to find?

To find the answer, we have to start by recognizing that people don't think the way they did in the early 20th century. Back then, societal affluence was a distant dream to most. We're losing the generation that lived through the Great Depression, but I wonder what they would think about American life today, and whether we've achieved true affluence.

The super-rich obviously have, but they always had it.

What does it say about the achievements of your society when you can regularly spot satellite dishes on the side of subsidized housing projects? What does it say when members of the middle class can own multiple cars and maybe even a boat?

There are nations on this Earth where it's a challenge to make clean water available. Even the poorest Americans usually take that for granted. There are nations where no decent medical care is available unless foreign missionaries show up and provide it. In America just about every community has a 24/7 urgent care clinic, and there are many programs available to help you pay for it if you can't afford it.

This is not to suggest that no one has any problems. Obviously people do, and the American economy itself has fundamental structural problems that could be the subject of another book. But by the standards of the world, even the poorest Americans live pretty well. We have largely achieved that affluence we were seeking.

While that's obviously a good thing, and we wouldn't want to give it back, it comes with side effects. Many young people have never gone through difficult trials. The generations that came before have largely paved the way for us to have an easier life than they did. This is not to say that life is easy, just that because of our ancestors' hard work and ingenuity, a certain comfort level has developed – one that could almost be called a "rut".

And even though most Americans probably suspect they live better than the rest of the world, they've never really experienced the world's poorest conditions. It's one thing to suspect it. It's another thing to have experienced both sides of it.

On June 20, 2013, a CBS News report cited a Mayo Clinic study released the same year that said more than 70 percent of Americans now take some sort of pharmaceutical drug, and more than half take at least two. Obviously, some of these are absolutely necessary to treat serious conditions. But 70 percent? How many of these are to deal with problems that earlier generations would have simply fought through, or dealt with through exercise or better diets?

And how many would have never been necessary in the first place if people had done those things all along? Pharmaceuticals usually mask or manage a problem, but they rarely eliminate it.

Many of the things we've done in recent years to try to manage our workforce have been like pharmaceuticals. They've either masked a problem or tried to manage it. They haven't really solved anything.

And solving this disconnect that sees nearly 40 percent of able-bodied Americans out of the workforce, is essential, especially considering the state of the U.S. economy. A fully employed, fully productive workforce would create wealth like we haven't seen in generations. It would unleash an economic boom that could fully fund the military, fund entitlement obligations, retire debt, rebuild infrastructure, make health care affordable and create a consuming public with purchasing power to make basic goods both plentiful and affordable.

Given the divisions in our politics today, people rarely agree about the way to get to the desired outcomes. But almost everyone, regardless of where they stand on the political spectrum, would agree that the outcomes I described in the previous paragraph are desirable ones. The key to doing this, before you worry about any sort of public policy, is to get the American workforce once again working at its full capacity.

Some argue that this calls for companies to simply hire as many people as possible, regardless of any other variable, simply because putting so much income in the hands of so many people would unleash some much-needed consumer purchasing power. But of course, it doesn't work that way. Full employment only gives us these kinds of benefits if the productivity is creating value-added wealth. So before you even put a person in a job, you have to have thought through whether you're putting that person in a position to generate that kind of value.

Does your production system do that? Does your technology support that? Does your training protocol lay the groundwork for it?

And perhaps most crucially of all, have you aligned the work to optimize the capacity of today's worker? Do you know how to identify that capacity? If we're going to thrive as a society, we have to transform our places of business in a way that soberly understands the available workforce – where they are as people collectively, and as individuals.

Crucially, this is not the same thing as pandering to them. For example, the fact that our societal affluence has allowed many people to escape some of life's tougher challenges is not a reason to make work easy. You don't say, "Well, people hate hard work, so we won't ask much of them." There's a difference between understanding where people are and catering to these least useful instincts.

But if you're going to get more out of your workforce, you have to understand their priorities, their value and their inclinations. Do they want the opportunity to be more creative in how they work? To make more of their own decisions? To use technology in certain ways? To work remotely or under flexible hours? Do they respond well to incentives? Do they need different kinds of support? Would they welcome certain kinds of challenges?

What are their long-term goals? What are their values? What are their issues? What are their deal breakers? Where are they flexible? What do they wish you understood about them?

What do they fear? What are their insecurities? What have they learned that's helping them? What do they need to unlearn . . . because it's wrong? And how do you tell them that? (And will they listen?)

What basic assumptions do they make about day-to-day life that are different from their parents? Or even their older siblings if they have any? Do they value traditional education, or do they think they've learned more through their experiences?

These questions and others like them have to be understood on two tracks. Each worker will have his or her own individual ideas. And there will be trends within the workforce in general. I'm not suggesting you need to make every employee fill out a questionnaire, but I am suggesting that we need to know people – however it makes the most sense to do that. Good research can help to tell us how people think and how they're likely to behave.

Then, once we're armed with that information, we need to find out how we draw up employment agreements that meet their needs and get the most out of them. When there are two sides to a negotiation, each gives some and each gets some. What do we need to give today's workers so we can get what we need from them? What are they willing to give in order to satisfy their own highest priorities?

And how can we design the workplace to ensure they thrive in it?

These are the crucial questions we have to answer. Of course, before we can answer them, we have to be willing to admit these changes are necessary. I'm not entirely sure we are. When humans are confronted with a problem they don't know how to solve, there's a natural and understandable response that simply denies the problem exists. It's less disruptive than tackling the problem head-on, and sometimes even if we see the problem we will rationalize inaction by arguing we're at a time when we simply can't afford the disruption of the status quo.

And when will you be able to afford it? Chances are, if

you don't know the answer, never.

I don't claim to have all the answers. But from what we've learned in recent years, we've been able to put together a set of practices and principles that has revolutionized our workforce and those in it. It's changed not only what they do and how they think, but what we and they can expect from each other. It's changed the culture of our work environment too. It's changed human relationships. It's radically altered outcomes. It's changed the way we think about the present and the future of our company.

Those are not small matters.

And we did all this simply by throwing out every assumption we had previously made about our people – how they live, how they think and how they work. We did that, and then we developed a new set of guiding principles based on what we learned about the realities of today.

I want to tell you what our company did, and how we did it. Because I think you and your employees will benefit from knowing about it. I suppose there's a risk I'm giving away a competitive advantage by revealing this knowledge. I don't care. This is too good to keep to myself.

I expect you're only a few chapters away from feeling the same way.

2

Employers, Only We Can Bring Them Back

As I write this in April 2018, we've rarely seen a tighter labor market. The government's official unemployment rate is below 4 percent. We all know that's not entirely accurate because it doesn't count people who have dropped out of the workforce, of course. But when you combine the low unemployment rate with the fact that so many people are not even looking for work at the moment, it creates obvious challenges for any company looking for workers.

But I want to challenge all those CEOs who are having trouble finding qualified workers to look to the future, and consider their honest beliefs about something: In five-to-10 years, do you think it will become easier or harder for you to find qualified employees?

Almost no one I know in business thinks it's going to get easier, at least not if the current state of things remains. So something is going to have to change the disposition of the workforce. The question is who leads that change. Does the government? Do educational institutions? Do social service agencies?

The focus of this chapter is my assertion that the business community, and only the business community, can drive that change.

Now, you might question whether that makes sense. Isn't the readiness of the workforce before it comes to us the real issue? Don't we need to lean on educators and training institutions to better prepare people? Don't we need to pressure cultural institutions to promote stronger families so there aren't so many people coming from broken homes? Don't we need to lobby the government for different policies so there will be more incentives to work?

No. We don't. All of the above might be positive developments, but they are not how you drive the solution to this problem. The business community itself has to do it, and we do it by thinking differently about the workforce and the very nature of employment.

Now let's start by recognizing that this is not such a radical idea. Things change and evolve all the time. Even if the basic structure appears the same, all kinds of details change, because people realize there are better ways to do things. I think others have embraced these changes more openly than the business community has.

Consider a baseball team. One hundred years ago, the team on the field had three outfielders, a pitcher and a catcher, and three basemen plus a shortstop. Same as today. There were nine innings and three outs per inning, and you had 25 men on the roster to get you through the game.

So baseball hasn't changed, right?

It appears that way on the surface, but in reality it's changed tremendously. Starting pitchers pitch fewer innings. Relief pitchers pitch more, and have specialized roles. Defensive alignments are more customized to the inclinations of individual hitters. Pitchers throw faster and have developed a wider repertoire of grips and speeds for their pitches.

These are just a few examples of how a game that is structurally the same as it was a century ago is actually very different. If video existed of a game from 1918, you'd recognize it as baseball, but it would look and feel like a very different kind of game. Everything from pitching windups to batters' swings to the way outfielders catch fly balls has changed.

That's because, as the years have gone by, people tried new techniques to see if they worked better than the old ones. Not all the new ideas were improvements, which is why you don't see a lot of Astroturf, powder blue uniforms or cookie-cutter stadiums anymore. But limiting pitchers to less than 120 pitches per start is with us to stay, even if it's not required by the official rules.

Things change. People who are interested in things getting better will embrace that change.

Television has changed dramatically too, mostly because it could. More delivery methods available to more people opened the door for different kinds of programming – some of which could never have pulled the mass audiences needed to survive when all we had were the big broadcast networks. But in their own specialized way, they're just right for targeted audiences who can keep them alive via cable, satellite services or Internet streaming.

New players were able to enter the game because the old gatekeepers no longer had the power to keep them out. They challenged convention, and by no means did they get everything right, but they disrupted the status quo in ways that have largely made viewers better off.

The business community by and large has been slower to embrace change, at least on the question of how the workforce operates. There are always incremental changes, of course, but for the most part we've got the same hierarchical structure and the same basic classification types we had generations ago. We still have blue-collar and white-collar workers. We still have your basic classifications of factory, farm, service, tech, construction and other groups. You know them well because they don't really change.

And yet people have changed tremendously – and that's true not only for our employees but also for the customers we're asking them to help us serve. People live differently, think differently and make very different assumptions about their lives. So why do we organize our workforce in basically the same way we did generations ago?

The simple answer is that the business community as a whole has not made a decision to drive this change. And only the business community can drive the change. Why? Because we're the ones who form the agreements with workers. We're the ones who establish the expectations of the workers. We're the ones who ultimately decide if the workers are succeeding or failing at their tasks.

The business community has to better react to what's happening with those in the labor force, but we can't be blind to the fact that they also react to what we do. Some of them may have given up looking for work because they don't think they can give us what we want. Some of them may believe we have nothing to offer them that suits their goals or their priorities. Some of them may think the things that are important to them are not important to us.

It's up to us to not only change where we can, but to make sure people in the workforce know we're doing so. And of course, it's up to us to make sure we live up to those changes once people become our employees – having been convinced that we really can offer the things that are important to them.

But with a few notable exceptions, the business community is not moving aggressively toward these kinds of changes. Why is that? I think it comes down to three reasons:

The first is ego. If you spend a lot of time convincing yourself and others that your company is great, how do you square that with a decision to make major changes in the way you engage the workforce? You're probably already selling your company as an "employer of choice" or something along those lines. You've probably already explored how to offer people a little more money, or slightly better vacation options, or marginally better benefits.

You're doing the best you can! At least that's the narrative in which you're heavily invested. A lot of people hesitate to make changes, not only because they don't want to admit they were wrong, but because they don't want to deal with other people giving them a hard time about it.

"I thought you said you were an employer of choice! Not so much, huh? So you were wrong, huh?"

Is there anyone more obnoxious than people who do that to you? But even though you know you shouldn't let them influence you, it's still no fun to have to listen to it. How many of us refrain from making the right move just because we don't want to catch grief about it? Or because we don't want to admit to ourselves that we weren't quite as good as we wanted to think we were?

Next is fear. Change makes you vulnerable, especially when there's a risk it won't work right away. "If we struggle with this, people will say . . ."

What will they say? Will they say you should have kept things the way they were? Will they say you were reckless and irresponsible abandoning the status quo? When someone makes a change and it doesn't seem to be working out, it's amazing how everyone claims to have warned you not to do it.

Maybe you're the CEO but you answer to a board of directors. Boards tend to be risk-averse since board members have a responsibility to represent shareholder interests, which will be affected by the change. The company embraced Policy A. They're used to Policy A. They know what to expect from it. Now you want to come along and get rid of Policy A and institute Policy Z instead? Why? Where did you come up with this Policy Z? What makes you so sure it will be better? Do other companies do this? No? You want to blaze a trail with it?

Blazing trails makes people nervous!

And indeed, it usually takes time to get to the breakthrough and ultimate success that proves the change was the right move. In the meantime, people get impatient. Some want to go back to the old way. Some want to get rid of you because you insisted on making the change, and bring in someone who will make them comfortable again.

It's hard to muster the intestinal fortitude to weather all that. Most people won't put themselves through it. That's how the status quo survives, even when the results it's delivering are not all that good.

The third reason the business community won't make these changes is simple denial. There really isn't a problem! Or at least, they'll insist, it's not so serious that it calls for any radical steps.

But just because you don't feel like there's a serious problem doesn't mean there isn't one. You might only feel that way because you've gotten used to managing your less-than-optimal circumstances. If I told you 10 years ago that we'd spend the next decade averaging less than 2.0 annual GDP growth, with nearly 40 percent of the work-capable adult population not even participating in the workforce, you'd probably have been horrified at the prospect.

Yet here we are. That's what we've been living with for the past decade. So why doesn't it feel like we've got a serious situation here? I'd suggest it's precisely because we have been living with it so long. You would never want it to happen because it's horrible, but once it happens and you can't stop it, you learn to deal with it the best you can. After a while, you've gotten so skilled at managing your way through it, you no longer think it's a crisis.

You might argue the same about the $20 trillion national debt. If I told you a decade ago that the national debt would double in only 10 years, you would have thought we'd be on the brink of a fiscal collapse. Yet it happened, and our day-today lives don't feel all that different. So is it really not such a big problem after all? Or have we just learned to live with it because there's nothing to be gained by worrying about it?

History is replete with examples of gathering storms that gave no clear warnings until they struck. Most of us didn't see the meltdown of the mortgage market coming in 2008. It happened quite abruptly and caught most people by surprise. Once it had occurred, of course, all kinds of people came forward and pointed to irregularities in the market that should have clued us in on what was about to happen.

So let me ask you a question: Given the serious problems this nation faces – mounting debt, entitlement obligations, military readiness, infrastructure that needs repair, failing health care systems, etc. – do you think our economy is productive enough to solve these problems strictly through economic growth?

That would, after all, be the best way to do it. If we could produce enough new wealth, we could draw off those resources to address these problems and others. A growing economy and tax base would offer the most painless path forward to deal with all this.

But if you agree with that, and I hope you do, let me ask you another question: Do you think today's workforce is capable of producing that much? Given the way employers are choosing to engage them?

I didn't think so.

And here's where we're getting in the way of our own success: Many members of the business community are buying into the idea that corporate America and its share-holders have become too prosperous and too wealthy, at the expense of the workers.

I recently attended an event featuring a presentation by a major bank's chief economist. I attended with a number of other business owners, and I was struck by how many were asking him some variation of the following question: "What do we do about the difference between the haves and the have-nots?"

They're serious. They were asking him how we can come up with a good system of transferring and redistributing wealth. They wondered if the government shouldn't mandate that this happen.

I think business leaders are kind of lost on this issue. They consume the same mass media as everyone else, and in spite of their own personal experiences by which they should know better, they're influenced by the constant barrage too.

They think the reason they can't find good workers is "income inequality."

This is half-wrong, of course, but the half that's wrong is a very big problem. Whenever someone doesn't have enough, earn enough, save enough . . . that's a problem. And yes, those who struggle to make ends meet are less likely to be good employees because they have issues in their lives that compromise their reliability, and often lead to bad habits. It's not a good thing when the people at the bottom of the income ladder are struggling.

The problem is in thinking this is caused by other people

having too much, as if wealth consists of a finite amount of money that never grows or increases in value, but merely gets passed around such that a dollar I gain must be a dollar someone else loses.

This is not how wealth works. At all. Wealth is a result of value-added productivity. Money is merely a measurement of it. And rarely have I seen it explained better than in a classic appearance by economist Milton Friedman on the old Phil Donahue Show.

Friedman, of course, was a renowned free-market enthusiast. Donahue, then as now, was someone who thought the rich were responsible for all the struggles of the poor. But he had Friedman on his show, perhaps thinking that he and members of his audience would be able to get the better of him.

They were wrong.

There were a lot of great moments in that appearance, which you can easily find on YouTube, but one of my favorites came when a woman stood up complaining about how there are too many millionaires. They can only eat so much, she explained, and when Friedman asked what she thinks they do with the rest of the money, she said, "They hoard it."

As he presses her, she admits that they don't really put it under their pillows, but they "invest it." She seems to have no idea at all what that means, so Friedman explains that when they invest that money in factories and other things, they're providing the capital that makes it possible for people to have jobs and get the things they need to live.

This woman didn't have a clue about this. She really thought that when rich people invest money, the money doesn't do anything productive, doesn't help anyone, doesn't lay the groundwork for anything worthwhile to happen. I'm not really sure how she thinks investors make money, but in fairness to her, there are an awful lot of people who are equally clueless about these things.

I wouldn't expect business owners to be in that group, but apparently quite a few are. Maybe this has to do with guilt. I've met successful business people whose consciences bothered them whenever they thought about the wealth they had accumulated. Maybe that's why so many talk about "giving back." Now, I like the idea of people who have money being generous with it, or using it to improve their communities or whatever else. That is absolutely a good thing to do.

But when you talk about the need to "give back," it implies that you took something that wasn't yours. That's not true. When you offered a quality product or service and someone was willing to pay the price you were asking for it, both parties got what they wanted out of the transaction. Neither one took wrongly from the other.

And there is nothing wrong with your having accumulated wealth. All that means is that there is a substantial amount of capital that you have the opportunity to direct. If you think it's best to give it away, then you can. If you think it's best to use it to expand your business, it's entirely up to you. If you want to spend it all on food, drinks and vacations . . . that's entirely your choice.

I suppose you can always have a discussion about which of these choices is the most morally superior. But good people should want to be as wealthy as possible, because that makes it possible for them to do all the good things they want to see done.

I once heard a pastor admonish church members who thought it was virtuous to live in poverty. "Why would you want to be poor?" he asked. "Poor people can't help anyone!"

Exactly. And struggling businesses with tight margins and tanking revenue can't hire people, nor can they pioneer better employment practices, nor can they give their people an opportunity to earn more. You may want to do these things, and they may be good things to do, but until you're doing well enough that you can put aside the resources for it, all you can do is talk about it and wish for it.

Think of the moments before an airplane takes off. The flight crew stands at the front and demonstrate emergency protocols, and one of the first things they tell you is that when that oxygen mask drops down in front of you, you need to put on your own mask before you attempt to help another person with theirs.

Why? Isn't that selfish? Shouldn't you put others ahead of yourself? Doesn't the Bible say that?

Sure. Helping others is absolutely what you should do. And in order to help others, one of the first things you have to make sure of is that you actually have the ability to do so. If you're fumbling with the other person's oxygen mask because you're struggling for air yourself, you might put theirs on wrong and never even get around to yours.

Now two people can't breathe. All because you tried to do something you didn't really have the ability to do.

Employees benefit when employers are economically strong and stable. Those employers may or may not choose to treat the employees well, but at least they are able to do so if they want to. Employers who are economically weak and unstable can't treat their employees well, even if they want to. They don't have the money.

So no, putting your company's prosperity first is not anti-worker. Some characterize it as corporate greed, and they use this to argue against free-market capitalism. Let me ask you something about that: Have you paid attention to what's happening in Venezuela? They're more than a decade into Hugo Chavez's socialist revolution. Things are so bad people are losing weight because they can't find food, nor is there enough of other basic goods like toilet paper.

How did this happen? Venezuela has a wealth of oil resources it could use to drive a prosperous economy. But guess what: There is greed in socialist countries too. There is greed everywhere. The people who have access to economic power tend to be the ones most likely to put their greed to work, which is why those in the socialist government engaged in corruption to enrich themselves at the expense of the general population.

Socialism didn't eliminate greed. It just empowered different people to be greedy.

In a capitalist economy there is also greed, but generally

speaking you have to produce something of value and convince people to buy it if you're going to satisfy your greed. If we're going to have greed – and we are – that's how I want it to work.

But look, greed is a dirty word. The Bible calls it one of the seven deadly sins. That's because it's talking about a simple desire for money and things strictly for the selfish benefit of the owner. The woman who got schooled by Milton Friedman on Donahue couldn't conceive of there being any other reason someone would want to get rich. To her, it's all greed.

I am not advocating greed. What I'm advocating is the embrace of prosperity that's born of productivity. The business that does well because it's very efficient at producing good things will positively impact its own bottom line, as well as the economic fortunes of its employees and its customers' quality of life.

A company that wants to be prosperous needs a workforce that can produce. That means hiring the right people, but that's only the start. And the truth is that many companies struggle so much with that first part that they never even get to the more challenging steps.

There are all kinds of books that will tell you how important it is to hire the right people. They'll encourage you to devote resources to doing so. They're not wrong about that, but where do you find the resources that tell you how to do it? You can hire personnel consultants who will help you administer aptitude tests or analyze resumes to see if you can identify the right fit.

But maybe we're doing this whole thing backwards. Maybe it's not about going out, finding the right people, convincing them to come work for you and then trying to make them fit into your system. Maybe it's the other way around. Maybe it's about designing a system that puts them in a position to succeed – one in which they can envision their own success and see their way clear to achieve it.

Also, maybe it's a system in which the employee sees the clear connection between his/her own productivity and the mutual success of him/her and the company.

How often have you heard in recent years that worker productivity is up, but wages are stagnant? In theory this should be impossible, because productivity should lead to prosperity, which should result in rewards for everyone involved.

How to explain this? A popular theory is that corporations are simply greedy, hoarding all the profits for themselves and refusing to give well-earned raises to their workers. You can see how that theory would be convincing to people who don't understand the labor market.

But if you do understand the labor market, then you know that you can't just keep lowballing workers on their wages and expect them to stick around and give you the same productivity. They might for a short period of time, but if you keep asking more of them and don't reward them for it, they'll find someone else who will pay them what they're actually worth.

And once you're dealing with significant turnover as a result of your unwillingness to pay people what they're worth, you're going to lose the productivity as well. Because any CEO can tell you a constantly churning workforce with high turnover is not a productive one.

No, that's not the reason wages are failing to keep up with productivity. The reason is we haven't got our people producing within a system that optimizes the value of what they're producing. That's because it's been generations since we've re-thought how the workplace should function.

Only business can do this. Only we can change the systems in which we ask people to operate. Only we can change the incentives we hope will spur our people to produce greater value. Only we can provide the tools and guidance they need to succeed. Only we can examine the workforce as it is today and offer the environment that would provide the ideal setting for their success.

And only we can give the 40 percent that have dropped out of the workforce a reason to return to it.

Why else would they? They've bailed because they see no advantage for themselves to being part of it. Now, many of them might be wrong about that. It's easy to argue that any sort of work is better than no work. I would probably take that position myself.

But if you decide to take a job that's less than the one you'd really want, you probably hope it's only a stepping stone to something truly rewarding and fulfilling. What if you don't see the business community in general offering you a path to something like that? What if you're convinced that the low-paying, unfulfilling job you're going to settle for is the one you're going to be stuck in for the rest of your life?

This is not intended as a defense of anyone's decision not to work. It's simply an attempt to get inside the head of the person who's made that decision. A business community that re-orients itself to suit today's workforce still won't lure everyone back. Some people have negative, defeatist attitudes and won't respond positively to anything. We can't change those people no matter what we do.

But an awful lot of what makes the difference happens on the margins. An awful lot of people would come to work if they thought there was a real reward, and a real future, involved in doing so. They don't see that right now, but they're open to it.

These are the people we need to put back to work. If we can, the productivity we can unleash would bring about a prosperity explosion that would transform the economic future of this nation.

A transformation like that is desperately needed, by the way. And yes, the business community is where it has to start. Now let's explore in more detail what kinds of jobs have been lost, so we can better define the necessary action steps to address the problem.

3

Three Kinds of Disaffected Worker

Before we can get people back into the workforce, it's important to understand who they are and why they've left it. There's always some danger in categorizing people, because millions of them will have their own individual issues and reasons for the choices they make.

But from my experience we can generally characterize those who have left the workforce by looking at them as members of three distinctive groups. If we understand and address the issues of all three of these groups, we may not get everyone back, but we'll achieve a massive and positive change.

Let's look at who these people are:

The Disenfranchised. A person who is disenfranchised either doesn't know how to function effectively within the workforce or, in many cases, has no interest in doing the things that would make this possible. They may be talented, but they don't know how to apply their talents, or how to manage their personal behavior or habits.

When we use the term "disenfranchised" we often think of people who have been unwillingly excluded from something by others, but that's not always the case. Sometimes you disenfranchise yourself with your own choices or attitudes. Sometimes the behavior you learn from your environment causes you to become disenfranchised.

But regardless of whose fault this is, we need to understand what disenfranchisement looks like in this context.

I had a buddy in high school who was not dumb by any means, but he did not receive good grades. His younger brothers did much better than he did, but they were not any smarter than he was. How did he explain his relative lack of performance?

He said, not without some justification, that public schools were set up to cater only to a certain kind of person, with a certain kind of learning style. (He tended to downplay the impact of his pot smoking.)

But did he have a point about the nature of the public schools? Sure. He had a point. I'm sure you've known kids whose grades didn't reflect their real intelligence, and might have struggled to fit into the one-size-fits-all learning structure of the public schools. That's something the education system should look at just as the business community should.

Having said that, let's be honest about something else: He tended to use this as an excuse. Just because it's not as easy or natural as you'd prefer to work within a given system does not relieve you of the obligation to try. A person who really wants to succeed will navigate that difficult terrain and find a way to achieve, even if the system in which he has to operate is not optimal for him.

It might still be true that he would do far better in a system that was custom-designed for him, but everyone cannot be educated in such a system. Nor can everyone be employed in such a system. Life doesn't work that way.

Whatever may be wrong with the educational structure, the person who can learn to succeed in it shows a high aptitude for being able to work well as a member of a team. Guess what? Just about every workplace will require you to work as part of a team. Even if you can convince a prospective employer that you had a 2.0 grade-point average because your school didn't cater to your particular learning style, what's going to happen when your employer doesn't cater to your particular work style?

Are you going to explain to your boss that you'd be performing much better if only his production system was better aligned with your work style? At some point you have to either become self-employed or learn to adapt.

And while I would agree that a one-size-fits-all work environment is as foolish as a one-size-fits-all learning environment, the truth is that not every disenfranchised person can really claim to have encountered that problem. Some have completely unrealistic expectations of what the workplace should be like for them.

Much of this owes to technology, social media and culture. Look around and you can absolutely find examples of 21-year-old tech moguls who've made it big. (And kudos to them for doing so.) Whether they've figured out how to sell like crazy on Amazon, or they developed an amazing app that everyone is downloading, or they connected the public to something it didn't even know it needed, these young people achieved quick success in a way that simply wouldn't have been possible a generation ago.

I have nothing but admiration for them. Who wouldn't do that if they could?

But culturally, there's a downside to this phenomenon. People in their 20s used to simply accept that they would have to start at the bottom of the ladder and work their way up. No one was going to simply going to become the CEO of a company without putting in years, learning the ropes, earning promotions and eventually reaching the executive level in their 40s or 50s if they really did well. It was simply understood that this was how it worked.

Today, because there are so many high-profile examples of 20-something millionaires, other 20-somethings can often get the impression that it's no longer necessary for any of them to work their way up, or to start at the bottom. In fact, the professional world hasn't changed that much for most people. The spectacular exceptions to the rule are a little more high-profile than they used to be, and maybe it's a little easier for you to imagine, "I could do that on the Internet too!"

But odds are you'll have to start out at the bottom and prove yourself. These days there are far too many young people who think that's beneath them, and because they think this, they have effectively disenfranchised themselves.

What we see on social media also tends to give us a false impression of how other people live. Let's say you have 500 Facebook friends. There are 52 weeks in the year so on average you'll have 10 friends on vacation every week, and at least a few of them will be posting pictures of themselves from the beach, Disney World or wherever they are.

You see this constantly and it leaves the subtle impression in your mind: My friends are always on vacation!

No, they're not. Fifty-one weeks a year they're sitting

at cubicles and not posting photos of it on Facebook. But it feels this way to you, and if you're not careful you can start to resent the whole idea of being at work. You can lose sight of the fact that work is part of your life, rather than something taking away from your life, and soon you find yourself wanting no part of it.

You've disenfranchised yourself because you reacted emotionally to impressions you got rather than engaging in critical thinking.

A lot of these people have been effectively disenfranchised their entire lives. They may have been black sheep in their own family – not entirely ostracized perhaps, but never quite fitting in with the norms and traditions that the rest of the family found easy to embrace. The fact that they struggle to fit in at school is no surprise, because they struggle to fit in everywhere.

Now look, there's a lot to be said for independent-mindedness. I wouldn't have been singing the praises of Henry Ford earlier in this book if I didn't think so. Sometimes the people who just never seem to fit in have to learn to view that as a strength and pursue something that challenges existing norms. There's nothing wrong with that at all.

But if you're going to try to make it in the established workplace, then you have to be able to do things as you're asked to do them.

That, of course, raises the question for employers: Have we become so rigid in the way we set up our workplaces that we make it too difficult for the disenfranchised to fit in? I believe we have, and in an upcoming chapter I'll expand on how our company has made adjustments to try to improve on this score.

I am not saying that every disenfranchised employee can be made successful by changes the company makes. Consider the case of Charlie Sheen when he was playing the lead on "Two And A Half Men." No one questions Sheen's acting ability or his star power. But we all heard the stories of his erratic behavior, his substance abuse and his tendency not to show up on set when the rest of the cast and crew were waiting for him. That was not the fault of the producers. If you can't show up, can't act professionally and can't stay sober, it doesn't matter how talented you are. You're making it harder for your employer to succeed and you're probably not going to have your job for long.

There is nothing employers can or should change for the benefit of people like that. They simply have to get their acts together.

But most people who are disenfranchised are not like that. They're basically following the typical human instinct that seeks to maximize pleasure and minimize pain. That applies both literally and figuratively. It can apply to actual physical pain, but it can also apply to the effort we decide is worthwhile to live the lives we want to live.

Somewhere along the line, too many people decided work was too much pain to be worth whatever pleasure it allows for. I'm not saying they're all correct about that, but that's how they become disenfranchised. We have to understand that if we hope to respond effectively to it.

The Sons and Daughters of Dysfunction. "Seinfeld" fans will remember how excited George Costanza was when he got hired by Kruger Industrial Smoothing – not because he was impressed by the company, but because he wasn't.

"That company is so poorly run," he gleefully told Jerry. "I could go hog wild in a place like that!"

George's goal was always to avoid having to work very hard. And he would work very hard at his goal of avoiding hard work!

But most people don't live in an absurd universe like this. Most people want to work for a strong, solid, stable company that has good leadership and clear goals – and where employees understand clearly what's expected of them, and have the opportunity to deliver.

Let's face it, though: There are a lot of Kruger Industrial Smoothings out there. There are a lot of poorly run companies that frustrate earnest employees who want to be part of a successful organization.

We have a joke at our company about what happens when we fall short of our own standards. It goes like this: When we don't do something that both raises the quality and lowers the cost, then we've let ourselves down, we've let our team down, we've let the company down . . . and we've failed our community, our country and God Himself. Otherwise it's OK.

The point of this is not to make people feel like they have no margin for error, nor that there is no room for mistakes, patience or learning. Rather, it's about how we define success, and what kind of determination we expect everyone to demonstrate in the pursuit of that success.

That's our culture, and our people need to see that, feel that and live that. At our company, it starts with me, of course, but I have to also make sure everyone else experiences and becomes a part of that culture.

Why is that important? Because without standards like that, we risk becoming the very sort of slipshod organization that loses its best people and gives rise to cynicism among those who remain.

And far too often, that cynicism sets in hard with people when they are very young, as a result of their very first job.

Everyone's experience is different, of course, and some people land spectacular jobs with phenomenal companies when they first enter the workforce. But for many people who are just starting out, and will take whatever job they can get in order to gain some experience, their introduction to the workforce is not so positive.

Maybe this happened to you. Maybe when you were first starting out you were having trouble getting interviews, or getting doors opened to you, until one day you found your way in to a place that was willing to give you a chance. You were glad to have the chance, but you quickly found out why that company tended to have openings. It was completely dysfunctional. Leadership was unsure of itself and had no clear, consistent vision for the company. Middle management had learned to survive by mastering company politics instead of by achieving worthwhile goals. Entry-level employees were overworked and underpaid, and quickly developed a negative attitude about their jobs.

Talk around the water cooler was often hushed, because it involved everyone's complaints about the company – or people's respective pursuit of new jobs. Be careful. The boss could walk in and hear us!

Maybe the company's leadership wasn't very forthcoming about things, so lots of rumors would fly. You would hear that the company wasn't going to make payroll that week. Or you'd hear that the boss was trying to get a big loan just to keep the company going. Or you'd hear that a major account was in jeopardy, and if it went away, it would be curtains for everyone.

And you'd wonder: Why did I come to work here? But you just wanted a job, and after months of looking and feeling frustrated, you found this. So you took it. It seemed better than nothing at the time. Now you were starting to wonder if it really was.

Congratulations. You've just discovered that there are some really bad companies out there. And for most people, chances are at some point you're going to work for one. If this is you, your experience is just like that of many other people. It's something to deal with, and it's not the end of the world.

But it does have the potential to become a trap for some workers. Those who spend too much time in dysfunctional organizations develop certain survival skills. That is understandable, but the problem is that these same skills tend not to translate to healthy work environments.

When accountability is lacking, or is uneven from one person to the next, people learn to play politics, or to take credit where they don't deserve it, or to make their achievements appear to be more than they really are. Or they learn to get the upper hand in intracompany rivalries.

Companies like this often see their employers divide up into camps. The longer someone stays in a setting like this, the better they become at working the system of the camps so they can protect their own turf and their own position.

And inherent in all this are the ideas some people get about the work world at large. If you spend long enough in a dysfunctional environment, you start to get the idea that all companies must be like this. All leadership is inept and insincere. All bosses are just playing games with you. All co-workers are out for themselves and not to be trusted.

Once you develop this type of cynicism, and take it with you into other work environments, you can become toxic to your new co-workers. These people are the products of dysfunctionality. It may not have been their fault that they had a bad experience with a bad employer, but they learned the wrong lesson from it. What they should have learned was how to persevere and do their best even in a less-than-ideal circumstance, while looking for something better. Instead, they learned to become distrustful and cynical about the very idea of work.

And a good employer who gets stuck with someone like

this can have only so much patience for it.

These people are effectively disengaged from the work world because they don't know how to believe in any company, any opportunity or any vision. And that means potentially good employers are paying the price for the sins of whomever turned them into such cynics.

That is a difficult phenomenon for the business world to combat, but we're missing out on an awful lot of potentially good people if we can't find a way.

The Automation Effect. A popular idea about automation goes something like this: Someone builds a machine that can do what a person used to do. The machine replaces the person, and there is no longer a job for that person.

That sounds very simple and straightforward. It's easy to believe. The only problem is that it's not at all how things work.

Automation does have a disruptive effect on the workforce, but it doesn't eliminate jobs. In fact, properly implemented automation will almost always create more jobs than it displaces because it enables greater productivity. It makes it possible to produce more wealth and do so faster. The net effect of that will always be more jobs, because more wealth will increase both the demand for goods and the means by which to produce them.

Automation is a net job creator. But it's true that automation eliminates some jobs while it creates others. The challenge for employers is to engage in forward thinking so we can reinvent jobs to respond to the opportunities automation and technology offer us.

Consider how information technology has changed the nature of the workplace. Obviously many people still commute to a job every day, but more people than ever are able to work remotely via connected mobile devices. We already know this has created a lot of jobs for people in the internet service business. But let's get a little closer to home.

In a four-block area of downtown Royal Oak, Michigan, there are four thriving coffee shops. On any given weekday, it would take you 10 or 15 minutes to walk around and visit each one. You'll find that each one is packed with people who are not only eating wraps and drinking coffee, but doing their professional work there.

Now, you might ask, what's the value of creating a bunch of barista jobs? Well, aside from the fact that those barista jobs just might be early career-starters for the people who have them (or they might help that barista get through college), you've increased the population of the downtown area by hundreds of people every day. That will also add to the viability of the other shops and restaurants in that city. It's one thing to have bars that attract people at night and on the weekends, but when you can keep a downtown area packed with people during the work day, you've really created an economically viable hub for a thriving community.

And it's all because so many of these people don't have to "go to work" in the literal, traditional sense.

Consider also the emerging phenomenon of online grocery shopping. Many of the major chains are now allowing people to pre-order their groceries online. They pull up to a designated parking spot and an employee will bring their groceries to them – for a small fee. This is going to create a certain kind of job opportunity for the employees who will essentially serve as surrogate shoppers.

But it will create other opportunities too. Online shopping is very convenient, but it does leave some gaps in the experience. If you shop online, you're not going to stop at the meat counter. You might buy some pre-packaged steaks or chicken, but if you like to pick out fresh meat straight from a butcher, you might augment your online shopping by stopping into a specialty meat shop.

That presents an opportunity for those who might consider starting such a shop, especially in one of those crowded cities that were ghost towns during the day before so many people were able to work remotely.

You see how this works?

Technology has always bred change, and the change has almost always been for the better – even if that wasn't apparent to us at first. Between the 1800s and the late 1900s, we went from horses to railroads to supersonic flight. Each advance rendered a previous technology obsolete, and forced people to adapt. But each one also made new things possible that had previously been hard to even think about.

Since then the change has been even faster. Robotics have already started changing the nature of work, but I don't think we've really seen much beyond the start of what robotics can really do. They will operate with more speed and precision than their human counterparts, and that will mean some manual jobs will be eliminated.

But because products can be made faster and better, and in greater quantities, just think of the opportunities that can open up. Talented sales people will have better-quality products to sell, and more of them. People who deal in natural resources will have more opportunities because manufacturers can accomplish more with the resources you can provide them.

And of course, someone has to design and build the robotics technology, and someone has to program it. Because of what the technology can produce, there is enough wealth available for all of these jobs to be supported.

And that's just the start. The more sophisticated the technology gets, the more opportunity it will present for people.

So how can workers respond to these changes brought on by technology? And how can the business community respond? Let's start with the workers:

I may not subscribe to everything Dr. Wayne Dyer said when he was living, but one of his observations was right on. He said the ego tends to tell people one of three lies about who they are: 1. I am what I do (meaning my job). 2. I am what I have – possessions and so forth. 3. I am what people think of me – my reputation.

I suppose that a lot of people who know these are not true statements nevertheless fall into a trap at times of thinking as if one or several of them are true.

So let's consider the first one. If you think you are what

you do, and your job defines you, then how could you possibly adjust when the thing you do is no longer in demand?

The person who was in charge of processing telegram orders for Western Union may have been very good at processing telegrams, and there's nothing wrong with that. But if that person believed that "telegram order processor" was the defining essence of his being, then he was in very big trouble in 2002 when Western Union discontinued the service. (I bet you're surprised it was still available that recently.)

In reality, you are not your job. You're a person who has any number of skills, and you owe it to yourself – as well as present and future employers – to discover as many ways as possible to apply those skills so you can provide value in exchange for money.

Here is where many of today's workers might need to change the way they think about themselves and their careers. You don't want to just learn one job, and be trained in that one job. You want to develop as wide a variety of skills as you can, and the more adaptable those skills are, the better. That way, when one type of job no longer serves society in the way it used to, you will have an easier time transitioning to a different kind of job – one that allows you to apply your skills in a different but still valuable way.

The factory welder who thinks he can never be anything but a factory welder is doing himself a disservice. He is surely capable of much more than that, and a more expansive understanding of how to use all those skills will not only benefit him, but can benefit both employers and consumers alike as he applies those skills in increasingly valuable ways.

So what about employers? We can start by raising up a workforce in which we don't pigeonhole people and rigidly define them. That might seem inconsistent with what I said earlier about my company's system of breaking down tasks into simple parts and training people quickly to do those simple parts. But I never said employees would be defined over the long term by only those simple tasks.

Companies should be encouraging their people to fully develop their skills, and should help them apply those skills in as many useful ways as possible. That can start with the kinds of people you're looking for in the first place. To stick with the example of the welder – recognizing of course that there is nothing at all wrong with a good welder – some might look at a hiring need as: "I need a welder, so I'll look for someone with experience as a welder."

You can take that approach if you want, but you can train someone to do welding. What if, instead of that, companies looked for smart, multi-talented people who would be interested in applying their skills and smarts to many different facets of the company's operations? What if companies encourage smart, talented employees to think about new tasks or concepts to help make the company more successful?

People like this will have much less trouble adapting when technology changes the nature of their jobs. They'll have learned from the outset to think creatively about how they can contribute. And they're much less likely a decade on to become despondent because their one job – the only thing they think they can do – has become obsolete.

These three categories surely don't cover every person who's left the workforce and needs to be brought back. But if employers can develop strategies to bring back the people in these three categories, we will bring about a truly massive change not only to the labor market, but also to what we can accomplish through the people in it.

Now, not every factor that's driven people out of the workforce is our fault. But why should that be our major concern? Someone has to make the moves necessary to bring them back. Why would we want to sit around and let someone else make those moves when we could drive the change ourselves?

That starts with understanding who they are, and why they left the workforce in the first place. You might have some other ideas about who these folks are, and if you do, those ideas would be a welcome contribution to the conversation. Hopefully I just got that conversation off to a strong start.

4

Who Not to Rely On to Solve the Problem (Tempting Though It May Be)

Perhaps it's hard for some people to understand why I say it's on the business community to address the condition of the workforce.

After all, you might argue, the 40 percent who have dropped out of the labor force aren't even working for us at the moment. How can we address their issues? Shouldn't the government do that? Or the education establishment? Or social service agencies?

No, no and no.

This is not to say that these institutions don't have any role to play, or that they haven't contributed to the problem. They most definitely have (especially government). That's a large part of the reason we shouldn't look to them to solve the problem. You don't usually put a crucial task on the back of someone who doesn't have a great track record.

But even if that were not the case, the fact remains that such a mission doesn't really suit the core capabilities of any of these institutions. Even if they did the very best they could, it still wouldn't work. Reconfiguring the workforce is not the sort of thing they're set up to do.

Let's start with government.

Obviously government plays an important role in the lives of Americans. But we often confuse that important role with the leading role. It's sort of like soil. Soil is very important in the production of food. When it's fertile, farmers can produce a good crop. When it's dry and infertile, farmers struggle to produce much that anyone can use.

But whether the soil is good or bad, you can't eat it. It's

not the food. It's just the environment in which the food can hopefully grow. And even the best soil can't actually plant the seeds. That's not what it's designed to do.

Government is like that. It has a very large influence on the environment in which we try to produce. When government policies are effective and friendly toward productivity, the producers have a better chance of doing well. When government is ineffective (or outright hostile toward business), it is much more difficult for government to be profitably productive.

And that's not what government exists to do. It exists to govern – to make and enforce laws, to build and maintain infrastructure – I suppose we can debate all day long what government should and shouldn't do. But you can't seriously suggest that government can be part of the productive sector of the economy.

And since government is so ill-equipped to do this, it's also totally wrong to think it can shore up the workforce.

Government doesn't make anything. All it does is take. (In the form of taxes.) And because it takes so much, it also has a lot. (Granted, it's also $20 trillion in debt, but for the moment we'll ignore that like our politicians usually do.) Some people think a government that has access to so many resources should be willing to give a lot of it away – enough, in fact, that people don't actually have to work to meet their basic needs.

Who is advocating this, you ask? Granola-eating, Birkenstock-wearing hippies? Well, of course, but not only them.

How about Mark Zuckerberg?

That's right. One of the richest men in the world – a status well-earned through his creation and leadership of Facebook – recently came out in favor of government providing everyone with a universal, minimum income that would meet their basic needs. This would require no work at all. It would be treated as a basic, inalienable right for everyone.

In a commencement speech he gave at Harvard in May 2017, Zuckerberg stated that, "We should explore ideas like universal basic income to make sure everyone has a cushion to try new ideas." Meaning, if people didn't have to worry all the time about how they were going to meet their basic needs, they'd be able to relax and concentrate on creating more great things like Facebook.

If you're a follower of Christianity like me then you know that when Christ walked the Earth, He didn't go around handing out food to people. He didn't even feed all the people who were hungry. Even when He did have his disciples turn five loaves of bread and two fishes into a massive feast, it was more about getting the people to stay put so they could listen to His teaching. (It was also about demonstrating His glory as the Son of God, but I can't do justice to the theological aspects here.)

Jesus was much more interested in showing people how to get what they needed than He was in just giving it to them. He didn't just snap his fingers and provide Peter a haul of fish after a night of not catching anything. He told Peter to lower his net on the other side of the boat, and then when Peter caught so many fish that he couldn't handle the haul, he had to get his friends to help him pull in the net.

Jesus was the most benevolent person who ever lived, but He didn't express his benevolence by giving people things for free. He did it by teaching them, which often involved showing them things they could do that they had never thought of. And He showed them how to implement it in their day-to-day lives.

Jesus commanded people to help others, freely and of their own accord. He especially commanded them to help the poor. But He never claimed there was any particular virtue in being poor. Being poor is a problem to solve. Being poor is a situation that requires help. And if everyone was poor, then who would have the means to help the poor?

No one.

Only producers can help non-producers, and the greatest form of help they can give is to help them become producers.

Now back to Zuckerberg: I think his heart is in the right place, but he's naive about what his idea would actually produce. He would take a subset of the population that's producing nothing, and unwittingly give it license to keep producing nothing.

It's not for no reason, by the way, that Zuckerberg suggests government undertake this. Only a non-producer like government, under the direction of non-producing politicians, would consider it for a second. They need votes, and it doesn't cost you anything to give them yours. No one else would consider it in their interests to discourage work on the part of others.

Now just because Mark Zuckerberg and a few others have advocated this doesn't mean it's going to happen. I see no widespread support for this particular idea. But the idea is treated by a lot of accomplished people as worth taking seriously. And while we're probably not going to see this happen any time soon, it still demonstrates something about government and how poorly suited it is to raise a productive workforce.

The instinct of politicians is to give things away to voters in exchange for votes. Remember, government doesn't make or produce anything. But if it can set things up where more people are receiving from the government than giving to the government, then it can establish a loyal class of voters who will always support their policies.

The instinct of politicians is never to tell people they have to work harder, or improve their habits or skills, or make necessary changes in their lives. Tell people that and they might not vote for you. I'm not sure that's true, but I believe it's what most politicians think. I suspect many people would appreciate and respect a politician who will give them the unvarnished truth, even if it challenges them a little. But good luck finding a political consultant who will tell his client to try this. So instead, we get government policies that seek to make it easy for you to stay where you are, and do what you've always done.

That is exactly the opposite of the way we need our workforce to think.

Consider: Can government provide health care? Of course not. Government isn't set up to do that. The only way government can guarantee people health care is by forcing doctors, nurses and other medical providers to do so under terms dictated by the government. We can debate whether this tends to work, but one thing you can't deny is that no one gets health care unless someone who knows how to provide it is willing to do the work.

The same is true of food. A lot of people think food should be considered a human right, and that government should guarantee everyone access to it. That makes no sense. Food isn't the sort of thing government has sitting around just because it's the government. Food is a product. Someone has to produce it. This wonderful nation is blessed with a lot of fertile land, but someone has to work that land if it's going to produce food.

This is where people sometimes suggest that government should, in effect, become the health care company and the food company and the whatever-else company. Government could employ the workers and ensure there is plenty of production, and that everything is readily available to people whether they can afford it or not.

Is this a good idea? Not a chance. To do what I just described would go against all market logic, and would inevitably result in shortages. That's what always happens when you deny producers the opportunity to make a decent return.

Look to Venezuela if you don't believe me. That's exactly what they're experiencing. Without getting into too much of that (it's another book altogether), I'll sum it up like this: Central control of the economy resulted in shortages of goods and public unrest. Today the stability of the nation itself hangs in the balance.

Government taking charge of re-tooling the workforce would give us the exact same result. It is not what we want.

There are some government-sponsored training programs, and a few of them are even mildly useful. But while they might teach a person a skill, they aren't going to change the way large groups of people think about work, their lives and their careers.

And if they tried to, honestly, they probably perform poorly. They probably would teach the wrong lessons. They probably would leave the workforce worse off than it is today. The right lessons have to come from the people who define and reward the work, and understand what is needed and expected from the workforce. That's not the government. It never will be.

I would even caution against the tendency to seek government funding for this effort. I know we all want to limit our costs whenever we can, but remember, when politicians pay for it, politicians make the rules. The business community knows what it needs, and has the resources to make it happen.

We need to take ownership of this from top to bottom.

Now let's also consider the possibility that the education community should take the lead on re-tooling the workforce. Makes sense, right? They have teachers. They have classrooms. Educating is what they do. Why shouldn't we look to our schools to turn the workforce in a better direction?

We've listened to presidents of both parties declare in State of the Union addresses that they want to see schools train the workforce of the future. But if you consider the real mission of education, you realize it's very limited in what it can do to prepare people for the workforce – especially if it stays in its lane, which it should.

Teaching can equip us with knowledge. It can help us to develop our skills. But what it can't do is give you skills you don't have. It can't make you a welder if you're not one. It can't make you a machinist if you're not one.

People often respond to issues in the workforce as if they are nothing more than training issues. "Let's send more people to trade school!" is often the cry. And when people talk about how college is "not for everyone" (which is true), the automatic assumption seems to be that if college is not for you, you must need to go to trade school and learn a skilled trade.

But that's making an awfully big assumption about millions of people all stuck into one of two categories – the college-is-for-them category and the college-is-not-for-them category. I'm not sure either category is really all that precise.

You can't make a person into something they're not simply by training them for it. Yes, you can teach people to perform basic tasks competently. But just because you were able to learn something on that level doesn't mean you're going to make a fruitful career out of it. It might be enough to earn you a paycheck at a point in your life when you desperately need to get one any way you can.

I am not suggesting that people should never take a job in the moment just so they can pay their bills and keep their home. Sometimes you have to do that. But if you have a vision for your life, that short-term job you had to take to make ends meet should be just that – a short-term thing. It shouldn't be what you do for the next 40 years.

Too many in today's workforce are just looking for any job they can get, and then staying in those jobs for as long as they can hold on. They're not thinking about the value proposition they can offer others in the business community and the world. They're not viewing themselves as free-standing business entities with something the world needs, and developing strategies for how to profit by offering that thing to the world.

This is the mindset the new workforce needs. And with all due respect to the teachers and other educators among us, they are in no position to guide young people to this way of thinking.

For one thing, most of them are unionized employees whose salaries are determined by collective bargaining, and who prioritize job security in the form of tenure and other civil service rules that make them difficult to fire even if they are incompetent. I'll dispense for now with my thoughts on that system, but anyone should be able to recognize that the mindset I'm looking for in the 21st century workforce is very different from it.

Either way, you can't make more mechanics by deciding you want to teach kids to be mechanics. That doesn't happen at the school level at all. If there's any outside force that influences young people's decisions in this regard, it's probably generational. You don't necessarily choose to do what your parents did, and you might not be skilled for it. But you've certainly been exposed to it, so you might be more inclined to choose that direction as a result.

And sometimes even "passion" for something doesn't mean you are meant to do it. When I was young, I had a passion for playing piano. I really wanted to learn to do it and do it well. I took a lot of lessons. I wanted very badly to be able to play, and I often thought about how cool it would be to entertain people, and to have big parties where I could perform.

But every time I started down the road of trying to learn, I ultimately quit. It wasn't for lack of interest. I really wanted to do it. But I found that passion to do something is one thing. Passion to learn it is something else entirely. There's a whole process you have to go through before you can be great at anything, and the learning process is often more demanding than the performing process. You have to maintain intense focus when you're struggling to understand something, or being introduced to a new concept and being challenged to master it.

Unless your passion drives you to excellence at all phases of the process, you're not going to excel at the thing you're trying to do. I eventually concluded that I had more passion for the idea of playing piano than I did for the hard work and discipline that would have allowed me to actually do it at a high level. That, too, is part of the process by which we discover what we are destined to do. And what we aren't.

The education system is poorly equipped to lead us through that process. It (meaning the process) should be self-directed. We have to choose a path and explore that path with everything we can, and find out if it's the right path for us. The education system that herds young people in groups of 25 or 30 through a prefabricated curriculum simply can't lead a young person through that process.

It also can't bestow gifts. Those come from God. I found this out the hard way early in my career. I tried to take square-peg people and squeeze them into round holes. And I was just good enough at it, applying just the right amount of pressure, that I could make it appear to have worked. Often the person being squeezed was far from sure that my plan was a good one, but I would keep assuring them that this was really going to work to their benefit.

It never did, of course. Ultimately I was being selfish by trying to force people into roles for which they were not gifted. I was trying to fit them into my vision for my company rather than giving them the chance to apply their own gifts.

There are some things, of course, that education can do that would help very much at building the business community and the workforce. One would be to teach people salesmanship. That is an art that many people could learn, and that could help them to do very well in their careers while bringing tremendous value to the companies they serve.

Sales trainer David Sandler used to describe a sales call like this:

"A sales call is like a Broadway play performed by a psychiatrist. What I mean by that is that you've got to be an actor who can slip into many different roles and you've got to be a psychiatrist who can see past the intellectual defenses people build around them."

How many young people are interested in acting, but never considered the possibility that this could be an element of a successful sales career? Consider the same about young people interested in psychiatry or psychology? These skills are gifts, and they could absolutely be applied to the discipline of salesmanship.

But that is hardly a mainstream element of most school curricula, even at the college level. There are marketing degrees, but not many pure sales degrees.

Why not? The reason brings us back to why we don't want to ask the school system to lead the re-tooling of our workforce. In the education community, there are certain avocations that are considered more worthy than others. I suppose if you're an academic by nature, you might have a negative preconception about people who do things like sales. It might strike you as blatant profiteering. And if you've never had to make a payroll, maybe it's understandable that you have a negative attitude toward it.

But the education establishment would do itself and the rest of us a favor to get over themselves a little and help prepare young people to enter fields like sales. There are an awful lot of people making good things, and an awful lot of people who might like to buy those things but for the lack of knowledge that they exist. A good salesperson can bridge that gap and bring people together, and can help make sure that the buyer is taken good care of.

As I said, your school can't bestow gifts upon you. But many students come equipped with the gifts that would allow them to be very good at sales, if only someone would teach them how to apply those skills.

If our education system would reconsider its curriculum in ways like these, it would truly make a solid contribution to the business community and the workforce.

Finally, let's consider the proposition that families should take the lead in re-tooling our workforce. I like the idea that your family influences your future more than anyone else. I want to see families encourage their children to do their best and to develop their skills.

Some even suggest that faltering family values are the root of all our society's problems.

I think the opposite is true. I believe that most things are downstream of culture, and even the prevailing family values in our society are influenced by trends in our culture. That certainly includes the breakdown of so many families, and the price their children are paying for that breakdown.

Popular media and entertainment constantly promote libertine attitudes about morality, and that's contributed to the disintegration of the nuclear family and the traditional method by which we have raised children. If there's a trend in family values, it's sadly reflecting those cultural trends.

But on an individual basis, families can of course do a great many things to help prepare their children for the work-force, and to teach them how to think differently about it.

I do wonder, though, if generational issues get in the way of that.

My parents' generation was taught that the best thing you can do when entering the workforce is to get into a big, estab-lished company that has good wages, a health care plan and retirement benefits. You get in, get established, gain seniority and put in the years required to collect on your pension.

Obviously there are still some people who do that, but as time goes on, many more people work independently, not only because technology makes it more feasible but also be-cause they've seen that some of those promises made by the big, established companies weren't all they were cracked up to be. General Motors careened into bankruptcy when it couldn't handle the health benefits of 100,000 retirees. And a lot of supposedly "secure" careers didn't end up so secure after all.

But people who were raised to think a certain way tend to have a hard time recognizing that times have changed, let alone teaching another generation about those changes. Your dad, who worked for the same company for 35 years, might have a hard time understanding why you've had seven jobs in five years. But it doesn't mean his way was necessarily better than yours. It might just mean you think differently about the value you're bringing to the workplace.

The career priorities of my kids' generation surprise me sometimes. I wonder if they've really thought through some of the trends they're following, and I note with some real concern that the younger generation seems to have a hard time understanding or appreciating the value of capitalism and free markets. I hope that as they get older and experience more things, that changes.

But there is probably a lot they're doing that only seems strange to me because of generational differences. If I'm going to hold my parents' generation to that standard, I have to hold my own to the same standard.

Ultimately anyone entering the workforce will have to blaze his or her own path. Family influence will matter, but nothing will matter as much as what's in their hearts.

And this is why no one but the business community itself can reach out and form the connections necessary to make today's workforce a productive, focused, prosperous group of people.

Government can't do it.

The education system can't do it.

Families can't do it.

Culture and entertainment sure as hell can't do it.

Only we can. We're the ones who will provide their professional homes. We know what's needed and expected of them.

The re-tooling of the American workforce is on us. And if we don't take the lead, those who do won't produce a result we're going to like.

So let's get started. But how, you ask?

I'm glad you asked, because that's where we need to take this discussion next.

5

Your Workplace . . .
and the Seven Personalities
Available to You

Have you ever had to take one of those complicated personality tests? You answer 50 or 100 or maybe hundreds of questions, and out of this comes charts and graphs and analysis that are supposed to identify your exact personality. It's awfully complicated, because it's designed to peg you very precisely.

"You test high for this and low for that, so you should be doing this job, and here is your career path."

To tell the truth, I always loved these aptitude tests when I was in school. I was fascinated by them. But you have to realize there's a difference between understanding patterns and thinking you can precisely define everyone for all time.

Can a process like this really peg a person that accurately? And are we making the whole thing too complicated to begin with?

There's a theory (according to theodysseyonline.com) that the entire human race consists of only seven personalities.

Seven!

They are:

Warrior. These determined people are always striving, never quit, and will do whatever it takes to achieve their goals. Second best is never good enough for them.

Sage. These are the entertainers, the people who constantly make you laugh and help you to enjoy life.

Scholar. Naturally curious intellects, these people are always asking questions because they want to know about everything.

Priest. They may or may not be ordained in a legal sense, but they're inspirational and visionary, and usually highly optimistic. When things look grim, they're the ones who find a way to reassure you there's a way to make it all work.

Artisan. The daydreamers, they're the ones who create the art and conceive the big ideas that change our world.

King. Naturally assertive, these people usually end up as the leaders of any group, even if they hold no formal leadership title. They have leadership qualities and others naturally look to them to play that role.

Server. These are the people who are always there ready to help you out. They're accommodating and they enjoy looking out for others and their needs.

Now like I said, this is just a theory, but my experience with people suggests that there is a lot to it. And what that tells me is that, when it comes to understanding people, we have probably made too complicated what is often reasonably simple.

What does any of this have to do with the workforce? Simply this: If we really want to get the most out of our people, we have to understand what makes them tick. You can do that with super-scientific, in-depth analysis using proprietary processes and technology. If you want to. But you can detect some pretty helpful patterns just by talking to people, and listening to people, and applying common sense as you're paying attention to what they tell you.

Everyone has a story. That person next to you in school or at work who annoys you, or perhaps treats you badly at times, has had his or her own experiences – perhaps even tragedies – that set in motion those patterns of behavior. If you knew all about them, it wouldn't necessarily excuse the worst thing the person does, but it would absolutely change your understanding of them.

But how do you learn these things?

Most people know that song by the Byrds (which is actually based on Ecclesiastes 3) that says for everything there is a season, and a time for every purpose under Heaven. There's a time for people to open up about things and a time to keep your head down and focus on what you need to be doing.

We are all familiar with the idea of the over-sharer who is always giving you too much information. But at the right time, and under the right circumstances, encouraging people to share will allow you to learn a great deal that will help you to more effectively lead the people on your team.

Our company takes the time on occasion to get employees together for get-to-know-you sessions. These are always enlightening. I've learned that there are certain techniques you need to employ to make them successful – like calling first on the people who are most comfortable sharing. That tends to loosen up the more reserved people so that, by the time you get to them, they don't feel so uncomfortable telling you at least something about themselves.

What do you learn and how can you use it? You'd be surprised.

If Steven Spielberg was to sit in that room with us as we're listening to our people and learning about their stories,

I'm convinced that he could take any one of them and create a film that would leave entire audiences bawling at the end. That's because, in our own ways, we've all had extraordinary lives.

One of my favorite films is the 1981 classic "Arthur", which starred Dudley Moore. The title character was the son of an aristocrat whose family expected him to marry the daughter of another wealthy family – in spite of the fact that he was crude and directionless. The idea was that marriage to this woman would get him straightened out.

But an even more interesting character to me was the father of the would-be bride. His name was Burt Johnson, and he was played by Stephen Elliott. He has little patience for Arthur's nonsense, and the more you know about his back story, the better you understand why.

Burt never finished school. In fact, he didn't even finish fifth grade. He was not born into money, and when he was very young he felt it was necessary to quit school and work to help support his family. That gave rise to a hard, sometimes uncompromising personality. He was fiercely protective of his family, and at one point he flat-out tells Arthur he should stop drinking because he becomes unreasonable when he drinks.

You can look at a character like Burt and think he needs to ease up on Arthur, or on people in general. He needs to cut them some slack. But if you know what Burt has been through, one of the things you understand is that no one cut him any slack, and that he had to learn to deal with that – and even thrive in the midst of it.

That doesn't mean it was OK that Burt tried to stab Arthur in reaction to Arthur jilting his daughter at the altar (although the fact that he only used a cheese knife makes it not so bad, I suppose). It simply means that you'd better understand why he did it.

And if you had to deal with a personality like Burt, you'd be able to lead him much more effectively if you knew his back story, what he'd been through, what drives him and how his tendencies formed.

I'm naturally curious, so when I see that someone's personality displays certain traits and patterns, it's in my nature to want to know why. I find it interesting to discover the reasons.

There is something to be said for the idea that, whatever has happened to you in life, you need to forgive people, get over it and get about the things you need to do. I don't accept people making excuses for their shortcomings, or acting like they can't help it because someone did something or said something or hurt them in some way – and they could never get past it.

But there's a difference between excusing things and understanding them. If I understand what you've been through, and how that's shaped you as a person, I can better lead you. I can better identify your best role within my organization. I might even be able to help you overcome certain issues if you want to do that. You can't really help someone overcome a problem if the person doesn't want to – but a lot of people do want to. They just don't know where to start. Good leaders can help if they understand what's going on.

Let's go back to Burt Johnson for a second. In the aristocratic world where he operated, most people had been to prestigious schools and had developed high-profile connections. They carried the credentials that you picked up in that world. Burt lacked a lot of that because the circumstances in his life had forced him to take a different path.

So what do you do with that? You could regard that experience as a burden, and view your life in terms of what you lacked or missed out on compared with the people around you. Burt could feel bad about himself because he didn't have some of those elite-type experiences.

But why should he feel that way? He had to overcome a lot more than many of his peers, and it didn't stop him from considerable achievements in his life. In fact, he took his challenges and turned them around so they could become the impetus for a great deal of success.

Burt's life had been a good deal messier than many of the people around him. He could be ashamed of that. Or he could celebrate that messiness. Which do you think is the better approach?

News flash: Life is a big mess.

That is neither a complaint nor a declaration of doom. It's simply the way it is. The problem is not so much the mess as the fact that we spend so much of our lives trying to outrun the messiness – as if there's really a way to live life without it.

You're covered in blood and screaming your head off when you're born. When you die, you might have it good and pass in your sleep, but you might go out just as bloody as you came in. Many do. In between, you'll deal with job losses, tumultuous relationships, child-raising challenges, car trouble, health issues, deaths in the family, arguments, mistakes, frustrations and things you forget you were supposed to do.

That's why I say Spielberg could make a tearjerker film out of just about anyone's life. It's not because all this is so extraordinary, but because it isn't. We all go through it. But I become disheartened sometimes when I see the way people try to run from the messiness.

At a given point in your life, you're dealing with something. If you're young and in school, you're trying to get through it so you can get to adulthood. Once you're a young adult, you're struggling for acceptance as you seek opportunities and experience. Once you gain that experience and some status in the work world, your responsibilities expand. You might be dealing with a full nest and you're counting the years until it's empty so you can do what you want to do with your time and your money.

Then, once the nest is empty, you find that you're declining physically, or you notice that cultural trends are becoming increasingly absurd and make no sense to you. Work isn't as easy as it used to be and you start thinking about how many more years you'll have to deal with it before you can retire.

Then you retire. Assuming you're financially solid

enough not to have to work, your time is your own. Now you're bored! And you're not getting any younger or healthier. Now you're wondering how much longer you even want to be around.

I'm not saying that everyone thinks like this. Not at all. But doesn't it sound like a very familiar way of thinking? Haven't we all known people who have fallen into these patterns? No matter what stage of life you're in, all you want is to be done with it so you can move on to the next one. You're sure the next one will be better because it won't have the problems of this one.

But the next one carries more than enough trouble of its own.

This is life. Why should we run from this? What is the point of trying to outlast the problem of the moment, as if no more problems are around the corner?

Celebrating the messiness of life helps us to fully appreciate the experience of being alive. Everything that's ever happened to you – good or bad, easy or hard, successful or not – has been part of shaping who you are. Even the things you didn't want to do, or the places you didn't want to go, or the difficulties you had hoped to avoid, helped to lead you where you are today.

Disdaining any of it merely causes you to disdain the state of your life. Celebrating the crap you've had to deal with doesn't mean you approve of the crap. It just means you appreciate who you are and the travels that have brought you to your present position.

And it would help corporate leaders a lot if we could find effective ways to encourage this in people. The more willing you are to celebrate your life and your experiences, the less inclined you feel to hide any of it. That means you're not hiding who you are, nor are you making it harder for us to understand what makes you tick.

If we could understand that better, we'd be in a better position to find the right roles for people who don't necessarily fit into traditional boxes.

We see this in sports all the time. One of my favorite examples is a now-retired Detroit Red Wings player named Tomas Holmström. I don't think I'm being overly harsh to say that Holmström was a little lacking in the traditional skills you look for in a hockey player, since Holmström himself says as much. When it comes to things like skating and puck-handling, he was surely much better than you or me. But according to the standards of the National Hockey League, he was below average.

If you applied strictly conventional thinking to Holmström, he would probably be playing in hockey's minor leagues.

But Holmström's coaches noticed something. There was one thing he did especially well, which is hanging out in front of the opposing goalie and essentially screening him – blocking his view of what's going on in front of him so he's less prepared to block incoming shots. This is a very specialized skill. Not many guys can do it. It often requires you to take some brutal shots from the other team.

But because Holmström mastered it to the extent he did, the Red Wings could deploy him in strategic situations and make it easier for their better shooters to succeed with a shot on goal. The Red Wings had a much higher shooting percentage when Holmström was playing this role, even though Holmström himself did not score a lot of goals.

He was what's known as a role player. He was not a superstar, and he was never going to lead the league in goals or assists. But because his coaches paid attention and thought creatively, they found a way to use him to help improve the team.

This happens a lot more in sports than it does in business. The NFL makes use of guys whose only real skill is accurate long-snapping on kicks and punts. Baseball teams will keep a left-handed relief pitcher on the roster whose only real talent is the ability to get a left-handed hitter out in a given situation. His typical appearance might consist of facing just that one hitter, and then he's out of the game. But his success in that situation could make the difference between winning and losing.

Teams in the NBA have been known to keep a guy on the roster whose primary skill is blocking shots. He'll mainly be used late in a game when a team is trying to protect a small lead. I've seen guys who were well over 7 feet tall and couldn't score a basket to save their lives. But they could get up there and block that shot. You wouldn't want that guy on the floor the entire game, because you'd expose his weaknesses too much. But in just the right situation, that role player could help you win the game.

Why don't we do this more in business? I think there are several reasons.

First, we tend to narrowly define and classify jobs. If you look at a job posting, you'll usually see that what's expected of the successful applicant is already very detailed and specific. And that's before you even know who will be filling the job. We tend to force people into predefined roles rather than crafting roles to suit people's skills.

I understand it's difficult to design systems without some consistency to the roles people will play. There has to be some way to categorize what you expect people to do. But going back to Tomas Holmström for a second, it's not as if he didn't play a position. He played left wing, and he had to do all the basic things left wings did. But when Holmström was on the ice, the coaches knew of his particular skills, so they were able to adjust the overall game strategy to get the most benefit out of his strengths.

Business can do a better job here. We can think less rigidly about how we expect teams to function. We can empower floor managers to deploy people with more flexibility so one person who is very good at a certain task can make better use of that skill.

You will recall at the start of this book that I talked about a change we had to make in our own production system. Once we lost several people who had been highly trained to handle complex, multi-faceted jobs, we had to break down those processes into smaller pieces and train people to perform more specialized tasks. That type of system-wide change required a lot of creativity. It also gave us the opportunity to put people in very specific roles that gave them the best opportunity to excel.

One could argue, I suppose, that by sticking people in such limited, specific roles, you limited their opportunity to grow. But that's only true if you choose to manage your workforce rigidly. Just because your job today is doing one thing and only one thing doesn't mean you can't demonstrate acumen to handle more challenging tasks. Good managers have to be able to recognize those skills and do the right thing, just as Tomas Holmström's coaches did.

A second reason business struggles with this, I think, is that it's not always as easy to pinpoint the skills of a given worker in business as it is in sports.

Athletic skill is generally physical, so you can often spot it just by having your eyes open and paying attention. Consider that guy I mentioned above who plays in the NBA and is a specialist at blocking shots. If he's good at blocking shots because he's 7-foot-5, that's kind of hard to miss. It will at least serve as a hint that you should test him in the low post and see how he does.

Spotting the specialized skills of a person in the business world goes back to that whole discussion of knowing what makes people tick. It's one thing to notice that a person operates a machine very skillfully, or knows how to trim meat. But it's often said these days that we're operating in a thought economy, and that the greatest skills people bring to the work environment are intellectual ones. If you don't go through the exercise of getting to know people's minds, how can you really identify their specialized skills? This is why we have to do a lot more than just draw up detailed job descriptions and hire the people who seem to fit them best. That's not much different than my old habit of cramming square pegs into round holes.

Encouraging people's real creativity requires us to first get to know it, and that usually requires more time and energy than we give it.

I also think the business community needs to have a more sober view of the likely rewards of creativity. A truly creative mind can open up all kinds of possibilities for the direction of your company – whether that's a tweak to your day-to-day process or an entirely new way of looking at your corporate mission.

But being business people, we often look for a quick and guaranteed return, and that can sometimes be an exercise in frustration.

I heard recently that Harvard Business School was teaching that innovation usually results in market disruption and makes the disruptor rich and successful. That happens sometimes. But innovation only brings you success when the market is ready for it.

Consider the example of the disposable diaper. It was first brought to market by Proctor & Gamble in the 1960s, but it wasn't their original idea. The idea has been around since the 1930s. If you know your history, of course, you know that this was the height of the Great Depression, when no one was interested in disposing of anything if they could hang onto it and continue to use it.

The idea was great. But when it was first conceived, the market wasn't ready for it.

Or consider the ideas of wind and solar energy. In theory, they're flawless ideas. Who could be against energy that comes from an infinitely renewable source that's free?

But the technology to harness it isn't free at all. And as of this moment, that technology hasn't advanced enough that we can reliably depend on these energy sources. This doesn't mean it will never happen. It very well could. But it will require more advances than we've seen to date, so for the moment this remains a brilliant idea for which we're simply not ready.

Does that mean there's no value to these ideas? Not at all. Research and development is all about taking great ideas and trying to find ways to make them work in the real world, in response to the demands of real markets. There would be nothing to research or develop if we didn't have creative thinkers coming up with seemingly outlandish ideas – the sort of thing that could change everything if you could find a way to make it work.

The person who can think like that is a valuable part of your team. The task for business is to find the right place for creative thinking in its larger mission. Obviously you need people who can perform the tasks that pay the bills and generate profit today. That's one set of skills. Without it, there's no tomorrow to dream about.

But you also need people who can envision where you're going in the long term. And if that vision is always safe, always conservative, always risk-averse, you're limiting your future before it even has a chance to get started.

If nothing else, we can say from all this that companies have to encourage their people to think, explore and grow. This is exactly how God designed us to be.

A lot of people draw the wrong conclusion from the story in Genesis in which Adam and Eve get in trouble with God because they eat from the tree of the knowledge of good and evil. God did not have a problem with Adam and Eve seeking knowledge. He created us to learn and grow.

The problem was that God had set parameters on how and under what circumstances they should seek that knowledge. The serpent knew that God had forbidden them to eat that fruit because He was seeking both their obedience and their trust of Him in the manner of how they would learn. If the serpent could entice them to reject God's instructions and seek knowledge on their own terms, then the serpent could create an issue between them and God.

Had Adam and Eve rejected the serpent's enticement and obeyed God, they would have gained no less knowledge. But they would have acquired that knowledge on God's terms, and it would have been more trustworthy.

I go through all that because people shouldn't make the mistake of thinking God doesn't want us to learn, or to grow, or to seek knowledge. He does. He just wants us to do it on

His terms, which is really not too much to ask considering that He is the author of all knowledge to begin with.

As employers, we should be encouraging our people to grow and learn as much as they possibly can, and to flex their brain muscles just as much as they would flex their other muscles.

And as all this happens, we need to engage with them and learn more about them. We need to know what makes them tick. That's the key to creating a work environment that works for today's workforce, especially those people who no longer see a place for themselves in that workforce – and for all of our sakes, need to be shown that they very much belong.

6

The Immutable Rules of Work
(Ignore Them at Your Peril)

Before we discuss the solutions to the challenge facing us, we have to establish some rules. If you don't understand the rules of work and employment, you're at risk of trying "solutions" that don't solve anything.

That's the benefit of experience, and it's one of the reasons only the business community can really take on this problem. Only the business community lives this every day and really understands the rules I'm about to lay out here.

And there's not much I'm going to cover that will be controversial, at least not to employers, and probably not to many employees either. If you've got any experience with work, and you give it much thought, you know these things.

So why spend time putting them on the record? Because solutions must be grounded in reality, and sometimes when we get it in our heads that we're going to solve the world's problems, we lose our grip on reality. Or we start thinking that if only our ideas are grand enough, reality won't apply. It will give way to our brilliance.

No. It won't. The rules apply. What's more, the rules will set you free. The rules will save you from wasting endless time chasing rainbows, and will keep you focused on real, attainable goals. Knowing the rules is good.

So let's get to know them:

Rule 1: Jobs that don't add value to society are worse than none at all.

This is a hard one for a lot of people to accept. There's a notion in society today that if people are willing to work hard enough, they should be paid for it. Paid well, even. There's also a school of thought in economics, based on the theories of John Maynard Keynes, that paying people to do any sort of work is economically healthy because that puts cash in the hands of those who will turn around and use it to consume goods.

No demand, they say, and there's no point in producing any supply. So, pay people for something, but pay them. That way they'll have cash and they'll spend it to buy your goods. So goes the theory.

It sounds good. But it's totally wrong. In fact, it's worse than useless. The more this thinking is applied, the more you hurt the economy.

Remember: The figure we use to measure the economy is Gross Domestic Product. The word "product" is the most important of the three. The economy is about productivity. Not all work is productive.

Let's say someone sent you out to a yard where there was a neat stack of 100 large concrete blocks. Your assignment is to take the stacks apart and move them to the other side of the yard. Then, having done that, move them back to the original spot in equally neat stacks. Nothing else happens in the yard that day. Just this.

You work very hard and do exactly what you were told to do. You do it very well. The stacks at the end of the day are impeccable.

If you are the person who did this work, you might certainly feel like you earned your pay. And if your employer agreed to pay you to do this, then you have every right to expect that pay.

But the fact of the matter is that nothing productive was accomplished as a result of this work, no matter how hard the person worked or how well the work was done. Nothing is produced by moving things around and then putting them back where you found them.

What I'm trying to establish here is that there's a difference between hard work and valuable work. Only when your work adds value and produces wealth is it rational for someone to pay you to do it.

The people who built the Empire State Building – and it's amazing to me that this was built before computers and even before a lot of our modern-day construction equipment – knew they had created something of value. The same is true of the Mackinac Bridge, and the Hoover Dam. These structures impacted everything from real estate markets to energy delivery to supply chain logistics. Building them made a difference. Whatever they cost, they repaid many times over because of that difference.

Can you imagine the tragedy if someone had built the Empire State Building and no one used it? Or built the Mackinac Bridge, and no one traveled it? Or built the Hoover Dam, and it turned out it made no difference whatsoever? Can you imagine lamenting the capital and the resources wasted if that had been the result of these projects?

Thankfully, that was not the case.

But if these projects had turned out so badly, it wouldn't have only been capital and resources that would have been wasted. It would also have been something even more valuable – time. There is no more precious commodity we have than time. We have very limited quantities of it, and we need as much of it as we can get if we're going to be productive.

If you spend time doing something that doesn't make a difference, doesn't produce wealth and doesn't generate value, you're flushing a resource you can never get back.

But even having understood all this, you might still think there is some good in paying a person to do a non-productive job, because at least he will have some money to buy the things that the productive people make.

Here's the problem with that: It costs money, resources and time to employ a person. If you've spent all that and gotten nothing of value in return, you can never get it back in any form. And although you could have used that same money, resources and time to have that person do something productive, it's too late now. It's gone.

The more we waste resources producing nothing, but merely moving money around from person to person, the less wealth we generate. That's why we don't experience growth. That's why you don't see people's situations improve. The only way that happens is when there is more wealth, and more opportunity, for them to access.

And the only way that happens is when everyone who's working is producing something of value. Oh, by the way, when that becomes reality, you won't have to worry about people lacking capital to purchase goods. There will be more than enough.

Rule 2: In a free-market economy, all application of technology tends toward full employment.

Ask your average worker who sees the rise of automation, and he is likely to be very skeptical of this rule. I get that. Everything he hears is that his employer wants to use technology to automate his job and get rid of him. The automation will be cheaper, won't take vacations, won't need health care and won't ever cop an attitude.

He'll be out, no longer useful, and no longer able to find work because everything he can do, the machines can now do better, cheaper and faster.

And as automation spreads, you'll have millions of workers who will need the free money Mark Zuckerberg wants the government to give them, because none of them will ever be able to find a job again.

That's the fear, and if you think of your situation in a vacuum, it's easy to see why you'd believe it could come true.

The problem is that we've got lots of history to show us how automation affects the workforce. And the trend toward automation has never resulted in more unemployment. It has always done the opposite. It has always tended in the direction of full employment.

This is not to say that specific people aren't displaced from specific jobs by automation. They absolutely are. Nor am I saying that no one who's displaced by automation ever fails to find another job. That does happen.

But the broader trend is always in the opposite direction.

And it's not hard to understand why. Automation boosts productivity, which boosts the creation of wealth, which boosts opportunity. Remember, economic growth is merely a measure of productivity. Productivity creates wealth, which is what makes it possible for new employment opportunities to happen.

If you want to look at it in broad terms, consider the technology of 300 years ago compared with the technology of today. Make a list of all the things people had to do manually, by hand, 300 years ago – that are now handled by automation. You could spend all day on it. All those destroyed jobs should have left everyone destitute.

And yet, even in the worst economic conditions, 90 percent of the active workforce is employed. How is that possible when all this automation rendered people's labor unnecessary?

It's because productivity always leads to new opportunities. Some say the newly ubiquitous nature of cell phones has killed the watch industry, because people can just look at their phones to check the time. But there's a company in Detroit called Shinola that is proving otherwise. Shinola doesn't mass-produce basic, utilitarian watches because it's true there's not much demand for those. But there remains demand for specialty, hand-crafted watches on a certain scale. Shinola has created jobs and opportunities by catering to this demand.

It's easy, and completely valid, to point out that automation generates jobs because people have to make the technology. But that's not the end of the opportunity created by automation. When a need people have is met more efficiently than before, it eliminates unproductive movement and expenditures of energy, and frees up that movement to be redirected in more productive ways.

People don't just sit around doing nothing because automation is meeting their needs. They pursue new possibilities, and this creates new opportunities and more jobs.

Rule 3: There is a perfect job for everyone, but 80 percent of people are in the wrong job.

Human beings are amazing creations, designed by God, each of us individually. We're all gifted with certain skills and inclinations. Each of us has different interests. And because of this, it's not much of a leap to conclude that each person is intended to do a certain kind of job.

People who find, attain and perform that perfect job – the one intended for them – have a high likelihood of being happy, fulfilled and content in their lives.

That's the good news. That bad news is that, according to my experience, 80 percent of all the people who have jobs are not doing the job intended for them. They're doing something else. And because of that, they're far less happy, fulfilled and content than they should be.

Individuals obviously have a lot of responsibility for the career choices they make. You can understand why someone, concerned about being able to make ends meet, would simply take any job that's available in order to get a paycheck. Maybe people know what they would really like to do, but they consider these dreams unrealistic or unattainable because life is complicated, goals are hard to reach and you just need to pay the bills.

It's understandable, but it's still a shame. Yes, it's hard to achieve a big dream. But something being hard is no reason to give up on it, and the relentless spirit of human beings going after their dreams is something we've lost far too much of.

But employers have a lot of culpability here too. We have become far too willing to keep people in jobs that don't really fit them – that old square-peg-in-the-round-hole proposition – because we're reluctant either to disrupt people's lives or to disrupt the status quo of our own companies.

We tend to think it's cruel and mean to fire people. You're forcing change on a person's life that is probably unwelcome, and may well create short-term hardship. But setting someone free from a less-than-ideal situation can be the thing that inspires the attainment of that goal that's been waiting for them all along.

Take the matter of attendance, for example. Some people are better than others at showing up, every day, at the same time. So those are the better employees, right? Not necessarily. There are certain jobs in which this ability is crucial, and you're not going to do well in those jobs if you can't show up every day. But other people have specialized skills that are very valuable indeed, even if consistent attendance might not be one of them.

We could throw those people over, or we could come up

with new ways of gleaning the value from their strengths. That would require employers to think differently, and more flexibly, about how jobs are supposed to work. That's the sort of break from the norm we tend to resist. It's also the sort of break from the norm that always precedes amazing breakthroughs.

Rule 4: People need to love their jobs, or they will never be happy and fulfilled.

This is obviously related to Rule 3, but it looks at the other side of it. Doing your perfect job puts you in a much better position to love your job, naturally. But that doesn't force you to love it. That has everything to do with how you look at work.

One of the worst things that ever happened to work was the notion of retirement. It fed the mindset that work is a grind – an awful part of your life – and that there's nothing you should want more than to arrive at the day when you don't have to do it anymore.

If you feel that way about work, you're doing it wrong. You're not seeing it as a positive, worthwhile endeavor from which you can take satisfaction.

I think the arc of the typical career has evolved in an unfortunate way. You start out at low pay and with low responsibility, then gradually work up to higher levels of both. Then you finally reach your highest point, and suddenly your career is completely over. You're doing nothing and you're making nothing.

That makes no sense.

Clearly, people slow down physically when they get older and they can't do certain things as well as they used to. Their health slips. Their stamina slips. I'm not saying their work life shouldn't change to account for that.

But all those years have also given them tremendous insight, and if they knew how to attain it, a lot of wisdom too. The older worker would more ideally recede into a teaching and mentoring role for those coming up, or even for those at the apex of their careers. They would earn less than they did at the peak, but they would still have an income and they would still have a purpose that gives them fulfillment.

As it stands right now, far too many people look forward to nothing about their work life more so than reaching the end of it. If you loved your job in the first place, you wouldn't see it that way. Somewhere along the line we decided culturally that work is a bad thing and that people should hate doing it.

We need to change the way we think about that. Everyone would be better off if we did.

Rule 5: Our personality traits and inclinations are 80 percent formed by the time we're 6 years old.

Sociologist Morris Massey, who is now retired, put out a very interesting series of tapes that discuss how people's personalities and traits are formed. One of them was called "What You Are Is Where You Were When." His theory is basically that most people's inclinations are formed very early in life, and are heavily influenced by what's going on in society at the time these formations are taking place.

Before anything else you experience has the chance to influence you, certain traits likely set in hard because of the influence of the people around you – parents, grandparents and maybe some others who are close to you. Combine this with the experiences you have, the cultural trends of the moment and your own God-given wiring, and you're pretty much set on the direction for your life.

This isn't to say you can't learn, grow, change and improve yourself as you get older. Of course you can. Everyone can, and needs to do that throughout their lives.

But the essential core of who you are is determined very early, and in most cases, that essential core is always going to drive your distinctive identity.

Why is this important? Dr. Massey explored the issue in a number of ways. One phenomenon he discovered was that employee discipline could be more effective when older workers and younger workers were treated differently.

In the '70s, Dr. Massey found that older employees who had grown up in the Great Depression valued, above all else, the opportunity to work. Younger employees had a very different attitude toward work, and valued their time off.

As a result, he found, companies who needed to discipline employees got better results from suspending older employees, whereas younger employees were given mandatory overtime.

This same principle also explains why it's such a fool's errand to try to "train" people into becoming things they are simply not. People are what they are. And whether they're creative, or mechanically inclined, or analytical, or scientific, or athletic – that's established very early in a person's life. You can train a person to do a craft for which they are naturally inclined. But just as you can't "train" a five-foot-tall guy to dunk a basketball (unless you lower the hoop to six feet, I guess), you can't train a creative to be a mechanic. And you can't train a financial guy to be an engineer. And you can't train a veterinarian to design furniture.

If we're going to get the most out of our people, we have to stop fighting what and who they are, and find ways to harness what they are. That means putting the right people in the right companies, and then in the right roles within those companies. And that starts with recognizing that who they are was established long before we ever had anything to say about it.

Rule 6: You can't be an effective parent unless you are happy and fulfilled.

If your traits are formed by the time you're six, then obviously your parents will be among your greatest influences. So, when we talk about parents and families influencing the attitudes of new members of the workforce, consider this: What attitude toward work are you going to learn if your parents hate their jobs?

You're six years old. You've barely even begun to understand what work is, but you know your parents have jobs and they have to go do them every day. What are they like when they come home? What do they say about their jobs?

Do they act exasperated? Do they complain about the work? The boss? The hours? The pay? Do they lament that they have to go back the following day? When the weekend comes, do they act like they've been paroled from prison? When Monday comes, do they look like they're headed off to the gallows?

This is what you observe in your parents' behavior. You're six. You don't really know what all of it means, exactly, or why it's happening. But you're learning to form associations in your mind. And if your parents always look unhappy about work, you learn to associate work with negative things. It's a grind. It's a hassle. It's a "necessary evil." It's long and hard and tiring, and the only thing good about it is when it's over.

Parents who are unhappy and unfulfilled in their jobs are going to communicate this to their children, whether they mean to or not.

The parent who is fulfilled and happy understands that there is value to work. And that parent is much more likely to teach his or her children that work has value – that it's a path to something better.

We talk a lot about poverty in our society, and we tend to define poverty in monetary terms. But poverty is a mindset as much as anything else. Those trapped in the poverty mindset sometimes learn to work the system, but they never really learn how to see work as an opportunity, as a way to climb to a better life.

When parents learn to be happy and fulfilled in their work, they are escaping the poverty mindset. And when that fulfillment leads them to believe their children will ultimately do even better than they have, they're free of it.

Rule 7: The family is a microcosm of all business, social and governmental organizations.

You name it, you deal with it in the professional world. Conflicts between people. Rules and the consequences of breaking them. Tragedy. Growth. Decision-making. Change that's as inevitable as the passing of time.

And chances are, the first time you deal with any of it in the professional world, it's not the first time you've dealt with it. Not if you grew up as part of a family.

In their own way, and on their own scale, families serve as the quintessential business, social organization or governmental entity. They're a child's first employer. Parents are the first mayors, governors or presidents you know – and the first CEOs. They're the first welfare organization that helps you (hopefully in such a way that you don't need a real one when you grow up).

Before you have a conflict with a co-worker, you're probably going to have one with a sibling. Before you have to ask a boss for a raise, or a promotion, you probably have to ask a parent for an allowance, or a change in your household chores. Before you seek more autonomy within your company, you're probably going to negotiate a later curfew, or more freedom to use the car.

Maybe you have to earn that privilege by mowing the lawn every week, or by doing the dishes, or by achieving a certain grade-point average.

And before you learn the hard lesson that comes from losing a job or failing to win a big account, you will probably learn the hard lessons that come from disappointing your parents in some way. These things happen in people's lives because they're how we learn, how we grow. Strong families, which can provide you with a support structure while you're going through this in your youth, provide the opportunity for you to not only survive it, but to thrive in the aftermath.

Most of what happens to us – good or bad – can ultimately be good because it teaches us. The best way to start learning that is in the family setting. That's where we can begin to understand how to apply it in adult situations.

This is why it's so crucial that families remain strong, and that parents understand their role beyond merely feeding and sheltering children. They're the leaders, the public officials, the protectors and the teachers. Get children used that, and they'll be ready for anything.

Rule 8: All organizations will struggle if they fail to address their highest-priority challenges first.

Every organization has problems. Some are big, others are small. Some create bigger issues than others. Any good executive knows that good decision-making starts with the ability to prioritize. Most people probably agree that you can't address every problem all at once, although maybe there are some super-leaders who think they can do it. I wish them luck.

But even they need to recognize that there are things called priorities. What is your most important issue? Why is it the most important? It might not be the one that annoys you the most. It might not be the one people complain about the most.

Your top priority issue should be the one that has the most impact on the organization's success or failure. It should be the one that affects the most other issues. And you need to assess that with clear eyes.

I'm reminded of the Stockdale Paradox, proffered by Vice Admiral James Stockdale, who is best remembered as Ross Perot's running mate in the 1992 presidential race. During his time as a prisoner of war in Hanoi, Vice Admiral Stockdale noted that the first of his fellow prisoners to die were the optimists. They told themselves they would only be held for a few weeks or months, and at first were very hopeful. But as the months and then years dragged on, they lost hope because they weren't prepared for the long haul.

The second group to die were the pessimists. You know people like this. They don't dare expect much out of life because they don't want to be disappointed. And since they don't hope for much, they don't achieve much. They died next because they didn't believe they could really survive under such impossible conditions, and they lost any will they might have had.

So who survived? The realists. These people understood that they were in for a long ordeal. They believed they would be free one day, and they steeled themselves for struggle. They believed they could make it, but they didn't have stars in their eyes about how quickly or easily the ordeal would end.

That's the attitude business leaders have to take in addressing their most important challenges. You can solve them, and if you do, it will have a huge impact on the rest of the organization. But it's probably not going to be easy, or quick, or cheap. Are you prepared to see it through?

Rule 9: Education and training are no quick fix.

Every politician says it. Regardless of party.

We're going to educate the workforce of the 21st century!

Whether they really believe it or they just want to sound like they're making a difference, it's an article of faith that education and training are what we need to get the workforce prepared for the challenges of the new century.

No.

Aside from the fact that the "new century" is now 18 years old, we need to get it through our heads that education and training represent no quick fix to the workforce – for all the reasons we've discussed at length in this book already.

The person who is really ready for the challenges of the workplace needs to start by being spiritually and emotionally healthy, on the inside. That requires strong and loving parenting. It requires the setting of a good example.

And it doesn't necessarily require some sort of clinical expertise on the part of the parents either.

If you've seen the film "I Am Sam," you'll recall that Sean Penn played a single father who was autistic. He did his best to raise his daughter, and his best turned out to be quite good. She was smart, good in school and well-liked by her peers. What he may have lacked in book smarts or in the ability to function socially, he more than made up for in his love for her.

There is a lot that parents can do to raise successful children, and clearly the ability to pass along good lessons and intelligence is part of it. But none of that is as important as raising children in a loving, healthy environment.

When young people coming into the workforce haven't had that, there is no amount of education and training that can make up for it. It can help to hone skills of basically healthy people, but it can't make them healthy and well-adjusted when they're simply not.

Rule 10: Effective organizations must master the art of collaboration.

Most companies will at least give lip service to the idea of being collaborative. Not that many really know how to master it.

The key to collaboration is a respectful, safe environment. They say that in brainstorming there are "no bad ideas," which I think people sometimes misunderstand. Obviously, there are ideas that don't make sense, and that you won't pursue for a variety of reasons. But the principle is that no one should be mocked, scoffed at or disrespected for trying to offer a helpful idea.

When the culture of an organization is respectful, that's not terribly difficult to achieve, although it will take some work. But when your culture is cut-throat, or passive-aggressive, people will be a lot less willing to freely collaborate.

That also goes for the way people are put into roles. You can be a very good person with a lot to offer, but a given role might not be a good fit for you. Organizations who understand collaboration will make adjustments in a situation like that – without attacking the person or making them feel like they've failed or let the company down.

Good collaborative organizations also understand the parameters of collaboration. Everyone gets a say in something. But no one should get a say in everything, because no one is an expert at everything. Part of good collaboration is trusting your colleagues in the areas where they have responsibility, just as you expect them to trust you in yours.

How you handle accountability is important as well. I'm reminded of the familiar scene from "The Breakfast Club," in which the principal confronts Judd Nelson's character and gives him detention for mouthing off. Judd's character continues to mouth off defiantly, and every time he does, the principal adds another detention. By the time the exchange is mercifully over, he's pretty much got detention for the rest of the year.

There's no reason for that. The initial punishment fit the initial crime. Once it's meted out, some people are going to handle it badly. But you don't accomplish anything at that point by piling on. Your goal should be to apply the necessary lesson and restore the person back to a good place as quickly as possible. All you do by hammering him again and again is release more negative energy.

What a good collaborative organization needs is positive energy. Get that established, and you'll be amazed at the genius of what your people can do together.

So those are the rules. We need to know them before we can apply the solutions. And having gone through the rules, it's time to do just that.

7

A.C.E.: The Answer

The key to unlocking job growth and workforce productivity can be found in three words:

Attitude.

Competency.

Energy.

That probably doesn't sound like anything all that revolutionary. They're all words we know very well, and for most of us they're cornerstones of how we run our companies.

But it's one thing to believe something is a good thing for your company and your workforce. It's another thing entirely to strategically incorporate it into your corporate culture. And to take it a step further, you and I can probably list 100 positive characteristics we would want to see in our employees. But all 100 of those characteristics cannot share space at the center of your workforce development strategy.

Employers have to decide which characteristics are most important and have the most impact. They have to choose the priorities that will not only do the most good, but will also have the most positive effect on other facets of the workforce and the company's operations.

The next chapter will be the one where I explain the nuts and bolts of how you accomplish this. But let's do as Stephen Covey would do, and begin with the end in mind. If you want to build a workforce that is productive, stable and sustainable, the key is to master attitude, competency and energy.

Let me elaborate by discussing each of the three in detail, then look at how and why they must go together:

Attitude.

When the New England Patriots were trailing the Atlanta Falcons 28-3 in Super Bowl LI, Patriots quarterback Tom Brady reportedly told his teammates to get ready for the greatest comeback in Super Bowl history – one that would be remembered as a miracle.

They got their miracle.

Thirty years earlier, the Detroit Tigers trailed the Toronto Blue Jays by 3½ games with only eight games remaining in the season. They had just lost three straight to the Blue Jays in Toronto, and a reporter asked Tigers outfielder Kirk Gibson if he thought the Tigers were through.

"Maybe," Gibson said. "Or maybe we're setting the biggest bear trap of all time."

The Tigers caught the bear. By the end of the following weekend, they were celebrating a division title.

A good attitude alone isn't going to guarantee you rise above every challenge. Sometimes you fall short. For every story like the two I shared here, I'm sure you can find many others where people confidently declared they would achieve the improbable – and still fell short.

But even if a good attitude isn't always sufficient to overcome tough circumstances, it's virtually guaranteed that with a bad attitude, you will succumb to those same circumstances. The person who wallows in problems, frustrations and setbacks – who identifies above all else with their suffering and unhappiness – is the last person you want to count on when the chips are down.

Everyone has experienced this: Someone on your team brings a perpetual bad attitude, or non-stop drama, into the workforce. This person's issues inevitably affect the others on the team, if only because they have to hear about them, or deal with them, or discuss them with others.

And most of the time, people's attitudes will affect the way the entire team functions.

Consider this scenario:

Ten employees are tasked with producing 10 work units each, every day. All do their jobs well and have good attitudes, so they consistently produce 100 work units a day between them.

But management decides it now needs the workforce to produce 110 work units a day, and the company hires a new employee who has a reputation for being a very hard, productive worker in the hope that he will bring the team's collective performance up to the desired higher level.

He joins the team, and he is indeed productive. In fact, he averages 12 work units per day. At first glance, the decision to hire him seems to be producing the desired results. But that's not the whole story.

He is also a drama king. And he's a complainer. Yes, he works very hard and he's good at what he does, but he gets into conflicts with his fellow employees. He finds fault with the way they perform, and with their levels of productivity. Even though he's not their manager and it's not his job to take them to task, he constantly makes negative, critical remarks.

This irritates the other workers, who often find themselves distracted by their reactions to the new guy's behavior. If they're not questioning themselves in response to his uninvited criticisms, they're talking in the hallway about him and the way he treats everyone else.

Now the productivity of the other workers starts to suffer. The new guy may be producing 12 work units per day, but the others – who had been averaging a perfectly acceptable 10 – are now averaging between 8 and 9 work units per day.

And the overall productivity of the team is now between 95 and 98 work units per day, on average. Although the new employee is productive on an individual level, his bad attitude is hurting the productivity of the rest of the team – and the overall result is that he represents a net negative. You're paying him to make the team more productive, but his overall effect on the team is to make it less productive than it was before you hired him.

Are there ways to deal with a problem like this? Sure there are, and they don't necessarily involve firing the toxic personality. At our company, we believe in approaching it by leaning in.

This is an analogy to downhill skiing. If you've never skied, you might instinctively think you can control your speed better by leaning back. That's how you do it in water skiing after all. But in downhill skiing it's different, and somewhat counterintuitive. You actually have more control over your speed and your movements if you lean in.

The same is true when people in your workforce present problems. You have to lean in and see if you can help address the situation. We'll sit down and have a conversation with them – not an accusatory one, but one that leads with an attitude of wanting to help. Someone who brings a bad attitude into the workplace is usually struggling with something. It might be anger, but that anger has a basis in something. If we can identify what that basis might be, we can try to help, or at the very least help the employee manage his or her negative feelings in the workplace so as not to negatively impact co-workers.

There has to be some firmness to this as well, although that doesn't take the form of yelling if you want it to actually work. You have to make it clear that it's not OK to bring a bad attitude into the workplace. You help if you can, you express your understanding and your support, and you make accommodations within reason to help the person deal with an issue.

But ultimately, they have to repay your willingness to be supportive with a commitment to leave the bad attitude at the door – if they can't release it from their lives entirely, which would be your ideal outcome – and take a professional and courteous approach to their jobs and to their colleagues, regardless of how they feel.

This won't always resolve the issue, but it can often achieve success because a lot of the time when a person is displaying unhappiness, what they're really trying to do is get someone to notice and care. If you make it clear that you have noticed, and that you do care, that will mitigate the issue with some folks.

Not everyone. But some. And that makes a worthwhile dent in the problem.

A couple of years ago there was a horrible video many people saw on the Internet of a young, female television reporter who was shot to death on live TV, along with her cameraman, by a disgruntled former employee. The guy had been fired from the station after a long history of violent and angry behavior.

Now there's no way to say for sure that a different management approach would have prevented this incident, and I don't know everything the station did to try to deal with him before they gave up and fired him. But this is a perfect example of what happens when an employee's anger and negativity fester over a long period of time.

If he was fired for his angry, negative attitude, you can be sure that during his time at the station his presence had a negative impact on his co-workers. When someone is always flying into a rage or just complaining, everyone else has to adjust their actions to account for it.

A problem for many companies is that, while there are people who are experts at diffusing such problems, they are generally not the same people who are experts at supervising the technical goings-on of the workplace. So, if the shift supervisor got his job because he really understands how to manage the operation of the machines, he's unlikely to be the guy who knows how to calm the angry employee. That's no knock on him. They're two different sets of skills. But you can't expect someone to expertly handle personnel conflicts or problem employees when it simply isn't their expertise to do so.

It's a worthwhile investment for any company to have members of the leadership team who are skilled in their dealings with people, not just with productivity and technology.

Fostering a positive attitude in the workplace is not as difficult as it might seem, but it does require some know-how and a consistently effective approach. If you recognize your workforce would be more productive with better attitudes and fewer people problems, you might give some thought to the benefits you'd gain if you invested in the management capacity to make it happen.

Competency.

When you think about competency, you might think about having mastered the tasks involved in a job. Or you might think about having been so well-trained that you have gained intense knowledge of what a job required.

That's all good stuff, and it's certainly part of what it takes to be competent at your job.

But I think of something else: Time. Or more particularly, the understanding of its value as applied to good decision-making.

Here's a simple way of illustrating the point: Let's say you want to buy a flashlight. A block from your house, there's a store selling the flashlight you want for $9. But 20 miles from your house, there's a store selling that same flashlight for $8.75. Leaving aside the cost of gas, would you spend the time to travel 20 miles (which means 40 both ways) to save

25 cents? This trip is probably going to eat up the better part of an hour.

If you would, then you apparently believe an hour of your time isn't worth any more than 25 cents. Or at the very least, you can't think of anything to do with an hour of your time that's worth more than 25 cents.

To put it in a work setting, consider an auto parts store that also does repairs. A customer comes in with a $100 part that's broken, and he wants you to fix it. It looks like it will be an all-day job.

Would you spend the entire day fixing this part when you could simply sell him a new one? If so, then you've just de-valued an hour of your time to less than $10. Imagine what would happen if that mechanic made the decision to do so, then reported his actions to the horrified owner of the shop?

"I earned my paycheck today!" he might declare.

"You wouldn't think that if you'd ever had to pay yourself," the owner would reply.

Competency means understanding that time is a limited resource. We will never get any more or any less of it. So, whoever uses it most wisely will go a long way toward the attainment of true competence.

Consider a race car driver. In an ideal world, you would complete the race without ever making a pit stop, but you know you're going to run out of gas if you try to do that. You have to stop some time.

So how well can you use that time in the pits? Let's say

you decided to do several pit stops. One for refueling. One for a change of tires. One for topping off your fluids. And yet another to have a guy squeegee your windshield. Let's say, on that last one, you decided to take advantage of your newly clear vision to check out some of the crowd.

You've failed the competency test badly here. You didn't recognize that, while you had to spend some time taking care of these issues (except for the crowd gazing . . . you didn't need to do that), there were better ways to allocate time and tasks so you could address the issues and get back to what you really came there to do, which was zooming around that track.

That's an obvious one that most people would recognize right away, of course. We've all seen the pit stops in which entire crews spring into action performing multiple tasks simultaneously, because time is the obvious difference between winning and losing that race.

I don't think most people recognize the value of time in their own jobs, though, let alone their lives.

Why so much focus on time in a section about general competency? Because competency comes down to prioritization and critical thinking. Doing well in these areas requires us to recognize the expanse as well as the limits of all the resources available to us – the tangible ones as well as the intangible.

The competent person must be resourceful. Given a set of tools and resources, and asked to achieve an objective, how well can your people do? Will they understand the most effective use of the tools? Will they wisely allocate the resources? And will they optimize the use of the time they have?

Many people don't know how to think of their own time as valuable because they've never been taught to think like entrepreneurs. That's a shame, because in reality every person who's alive should think of himself or herself as the CEO of an enterprise. That enterprise is your life. (One might point out that God is the chairman of the board, but you're the CEO.)

That means that every hour of your life is a decision you make, and comes with inherent value. How will you get the most out of it? What worthwhile goal can you achieve in that hour? This is not to say that every hour should be spent treating your life like a business. Relaxation and leisure are obviously parts of life too. Great parts! But there too, you're making decisions about time.

How much time will you spend on leisure compared with the time you need to spend earning the means that allow you to enjoy it? What is the right balance? As CEO of your life, you have to make that decision, and constantly check it to make sure you've decided well. You must make adjustments if the facts warrant them. It's your decision!

I once knew a guy who lost his job. Finding himself unemployed for the first time, how would he spend his time when he had no work to do?

Well, he didn't see it that way. He set his alarm for 7 a.m. every morning, got up, showered, got dressed and went to work . . . looking for work. He treated it as a full-time job.

He did it until 5 p.m. every day. This was before the Internet became what it is today, so he explored resources like business listings he could access at his library. He drove around to visit people who would see him.

And he found a job. Not right away, but he was relentless and, eventually, rewarded.

The key here was that he didn't accept the notion that he didn't have a job. He had to earn an income, and having lost his source of income, his full-time job was to find a new source. This was his decision for how to allocate the time available to the enterprise he led, which was his life.

The pursuit of opportunity, and of productivity, is a very high-value use of a person's time. It's worth a lot. It's worth a lot more than that 25 cents you might save going across town to buy a flashlight. There are a lot of other valuable ways you can use your time as well. You can use it teaching, encouraging, sharing and helping others. Those who show a knack for using their time in these ways usually prove to be far more competent than those who don't. They've shown they can prioritize and exercise good judgment.

Competency is about a lot of things – skill, training, focus, reliability – but I think above all else it's about knowing how to make good decisions, on a consistent basis, throughout the day. In my experience, the person who understands the value of time is the most likely person to demonstrate that kind of competence in other areas.

Energy.

I have a firmly held belief with which many people disagree. But I'm convinced of it.

I don't believe anyone is truly lazy.

When I say this, people usually offer what they think is plenty of evidence to the contrary. If it's not about people they know who sit around and do nothing productive, it's about societal trends that show too many people simply opting out of the productive sector.

That, after all, is what this whole book is really all about.

I know that all that happens. But I disagree with the conventional view that it's caused by laziness.

A lazy person, assuming one exists, simply doesn't care to put forth the energy to do anything. It's too much trouble, too much effort. The lazy person would rather just rest, pretty much all the time, I guess, because it's easier.

So goes the theory. But I don't believe that person actually exists. And if you really study the patterns of supposedly "lazy" people, you'll find that the way they actually live is not consistent with that.

They do expend energy. They just don't expend it wisely or productively. They'll expend it in response to anger, or fear, or the threat of losing something they think they need.

They'll also expend it in other ways. An OCD person will stand in front of a mirror for 15 minutes making sure there's not a hair out of place, or run back eight times to make sure the burners on the stove are turned off.

Lazy people wouldn't do any of that. Why would they care? However, you see people all the time who don't appear to have much direction or ambition, but they're expending plenty of energy. Just not in ways that get them anywhere good.

So, if people aren't lazy, how can we explain their disinclination to expend energy in a productive manner?

What appears to be laziness, I believe is usually rooted in fear and anxiety. And I've got a lot of years as an employer under my belt to back up this belief.

People will expend energy for an endeavor about which they feel comfortable or safe. They'll get up or go out to get some lunch. If they're offended, they might throw a fit. If they're dependent on public assistance, they'll get pretty good at working the system.

All those things take energy. What it doesn't do is put them at risk of failure, or disappointment, or consequences. And it doesn't force them to make a decision that might later turn out to be wrong.

I believe most people who appear lazy are simply gripped with fear and anxiety. It's not that they aren't willing to expend energy to obtain a good reward. It's that they're terrified of what will happen if they make a decision to do so. It might not work out. Something might go wrong. Someone might not keep a promise to them. They might try, fail and be humiliated.

And if they make a move that doesn't turn out to be the right one, they're terrified they won't be able to handle the consequences. So they freeze, make no decision at all, and ultimately just stay in place.

In reality, the ability to make decisions almost always

rewards you. Even the challenges of correcting a wrong decision usually pale in comparison to what happens when you're afraid to make a decision in the first place. Refusing to make decisions might occasionally spare you a failure, but it will also eliminate the possibility of many successes.

Consider the approach of pitcher David Price of the Boston Red Sox. Price is known for his ability to consistently pitch into the eighth and even ninth innings of many games, while the average starting pitcher usually has to leave a game by the sixth or seventh inning. Why is Price so good at this? Because he knows he can only throw so many pitches in a game – usually around 100. Price's philosophy is that he prefers to see a hitter do something – either make an out or get a hit – within three pitches, rather than taking many more pitches to ultimately get the hitter out. So he attacks the strike zone to avoid getting behind in the ball/strike count, and invites hitters to make contact.

Now, doesn't this put him at greater risk of opposing hitters getting on base? Yes and no. It prevents him from walking many hitters, but pounding the strike zone might result in some hitters making good contact and getting hits. Price figures his pitches are so good that he can usually get hitters out while throwing strikes, but if a hitter does occasionally get on base, he can manage the situation. And he prefers that to running up a high pitch count and having to exit the game early.

It doesn't always work. I remember a night when nine New York Yankees in a row got hits off him, and he had to leave the game in the second inning. But it works most of the time, and Price has become a very successful major league pitcher.

The key is that he's made a decision to manage his energy in a certain way, even recognizing that there are some risks to that approach. He only has enough energy to throw so many pitches in a game, so he has to use that amount of energy to put away as many hitters as he can. He believes he can manage the risks, so he's not afraid to stay with the approach that has given him the best results.

Pitchers who throw far fewer innings every year aren't lazy. But they're not as willing as David Price to use their energy as efficiently, or to manage the potential risks of doing so.

The person who is gripped with fear and won't make a move in one direction or another is like the computers of 10 or 15 years ago. You remember them. They could do some cool things, but they also had a tendency to freeze up if you asked them to do too many things at once. They would cause you to lose what you were working on, and you'd have to take the time to shut them down and reboot them so you could get them working again.

People who freeze up and don't move aren't lazy. They're overwhelmed. They're terrified. They're unsure of themselves and don't want to take the risk of moving from where they are.

I realize that often takes on the appearance of laziness, but I've never met a person who didn't want to improve his or her life, or wouldn't do something they felt confident would have that effect – if they really believed they could pull it off successfully.

We need a workforce that is not only willing, but un-afraid, to expend its energy in the service of productivity. We need people who are willing to make decisions on behalf of their own lives, and who can make decisions throughout the course of the workday about how they're going to apply energy to achieve the goals of our organizations.

Making this reality will require us to approach our work-force in a very different way, and we can do it. We can inspire the attitude, the competency and the energy we need from our people. And we can adjust our approach to how we do business, and how we hire, so we can bring back to the fold the many potentially good workers who have dropped out of the workforce.

I spent a lot of time in this chapter examining three char-acteristics I believe are absolutely essential to the formation of an effective and productive workforce. You can make a much longer list than just these, but I am convinced that if you get these three, the others will quickly follow.

So how do we do it? What are the ins and outs? What are the steps? What resources do we need to deploy, or redeploy? What decisions do we need to make and implement in order for this vision to become reality?

I am not going to tell you what I think the answer is. I'm going to tell you what I know the answer is, because my company has already done it. And it's worked.

8

The Five Pillars
(How You Make It Work at Your
Company)

Having identified attitude, competence and energy as the keys to developing a stable and productive workforce, I realize I begged the question:

Fine, so how do you make that happen?

It's time to answer that question in detail.

As I discussed earlier in this book, our company found ourselves with a workforce crisis some years back when we lost more than 50 key people all at once, as a result of an immigration enforcement action. I covered the details already, so I won't do so again here (except to remind you that we did nothing wrong and no one ever suggested we did).

We had to reload and retool quickly, and it forced us to take a hard look at every aspect of our team, as well as our employment and management practices. We wanted to make sure the new team would not only be productive for us, but also that it would be happy, healthy and stable going forward.

It was during this process that we developed ACE – with the emphasis on attitude, competence and energy. We came to understand that these were the three keys to success in our efforts to build and keep the kind of workforce we needed.

Developing the method of accomplishing it took considerably more thought and effort. But the method has been so successful, and yielded such excellent results, that it's really the reason I decided to write this book. I realize there's a school of thought in business that, when you come up with a successful proprietary idea, you should protect that information lest others steal it from you.

But the potential for these ideas to revolutionize the

workforce, and to change people's lives, is so powerful that I want you to steal it. Or more accurately, I want to give it away to you. I'm convinced that if the entire business community adopted this thinking and implemented these ideas, the resulting change in the workforce would be so powerful and positive that all of us would enjoy more than enough prosperity as a result.

It doesn't help me if your workforce is substandard. I want it to be the best it can be. And that's good for the country as a whole, too. So, let me introduce you to the five pillars of ACE, the tangible action steps that actually turn this vision into reality:

Recruitment and cultural fit
Onboarding and engagement
Supervision and leadership
Evaluation and guidance
Process evolution and fragmentation

Here are the details of each:
Recruitment and cultural fit.
We have about 30,000 applicants each year, for a couple hundred job openings. That's a great pool to draw from, but there's also a lot of potential to choose applicants who might be good people, but are not the right fit.

And to be more specific about that, I'm talking about two kinds of fits – a fit for the company culture, and a fit for the specific task that needs to be performed.

Finding the right fits requires a very smart and effective screening process. But that doesn't mean it's overly complicated or unwieldy.

The usual process starts with having management, and only management, interview people for a job. That may be your only option in a very small organization. But we find it's much more effective if you involve people who actually specialize in the task that needs to be performed. No one knows the job better than they do.

These employees also have a good handle on the company culture, and they're at a peer level with the person being interviewed. So they're in a good position to know if the applicant is good cultural fit.

By the way, I would encourage any person being interviewed for a job – whether it's with us or any other company – to interview the company back. The interview should go both ways. We're trying to determine if you're a good fit for us, but you should be asking the same question: Are we a good fit for you? It's no crime if we're not. Not every person is a fit with every company and we're better off finding that out at the start than beginning a relationship that goes badly.

A lot of job applicants are convinced they simply need to take whatever job they can get, so they'll sit there and try to convince you they're exactly what you want them to be. That turns out about as well in the workplace as it does in personal relationships. Eventually you reveal yourself to be what you really are, and if it's not what you presented yourself to be at the outset, things are going to go bad in a hurry.

I would rather see a person, even if they're unemployed, reject a company that's not a good fit and keep looking.

And we might reject a person too, because we're simply not convinced that they fit. If we do, it's human nature to feel rejected and not like it very much. I completely understand. But it's not personal. The applicant for a job doesn't usually know everything the company is looking for. Sometimes we want someone just like the rest of our team. Other times we're looking for a fresh perspective and we want someone completely different.

If a person doesn't get chosen because the fit was wrong, then we did that person a favor by not trying to force him or her into a situation that had little promise of success.

This is why recruitment has to be about a lot more than just finding as many people as possible who might want to work for your company. It has to be a very proactive process by the company to define the kinds of people who will fit – both culture and tasks – and to do rigorous enough testing to be sure.

We do several rounds of testing. We start with automatic screening systems from a major job recruitment site. You have to use a resource like that to get from 30,000 applicants down to a few hundred. The ones we identify as strong candidates get phone interviews, and from there we identify the ones we want to bring in for more rigorous testing.

Some of the testing is so simple, it almost seems kind of silly. But it's very effective. One test involves putting a stack of boxes on a pallet and asking applicants to move the boxes to another pallet. What's the value of that? A lot. We watch to see if they match the original stacking patterns, and how they approach the physicality involved with the task. We also watch things like body language, and listen to what kinds of things they say while performing the test.

This tells you more than you would expect about how the person thinks, and how the person approaches tasks.

Another test we have them do involves coin counting. Most of our general laborers don't handle money, but that's not really the point. The coin-counting test tells us about their finesse skills, their accuracy and ability to focus. All of this is relevant to what meat-processing workers have to do, so it tells us a great deal about who will thrive in our actual work environment.

Next, we have them play a game. You may have played it yourself at some point. It's called Perfection – the game in which you have to put all the differently shaped pieces into the corresponding holes and hit the timer before it goes off and the whole thing pops up.

We learn a lot about people from the way they play this game, not least the number of times I've seen people sit there and argue with the pieces because they're convinced they should go into a space where they clearly don't fit. Perfection tells us a lot about how people respond when under pressure, even if we're only talking about the pressure of a game with a clock.

I'd rather find out from a game that they struggle with this than find out from a workplace accident or a major mishap.

By the way, in the course of this process, here's something I hear a lot: I'm a really good worker, I'm just not good at taking tests.

Sorry. The test is designed to show how you can handle the same kinds of challenges that would present themselves on the job. It makes no sense for me to hire people who perform the tests poorly when I've got people who performed them well. And I've never had a result that made me doubt that principle.

If you're bad at the things we're testing you in, you're going to be bad at the job. That's why we're both better off for having gone through the test and seen the results. This person needs to pursue a job that's a good fit.

We also put applicants through the classic DISC profile to measure dominance, influence, steadiness and conscientiousness. This is not the sort of test where there are right or wrong answers, but they tell us about the type of personality we're getting. That's crucial in determining whether the fit is good or bad.

All this happens before we even start with aptitude testing, where we test them on things like common software and other proficiencies – depending on the nature of the job.

By the time we've been through all this, we've got a pretty good idea of whether a potential employee will fit, do the job well and last as a long-term employee.

I realize that some CEOs might read this and question whether the effort is really worth it for their companies. They might consider the work their employees do too simple to justify such extensive testing. And I can understand resisting a process that will reject so many people, because it does make the hiring process a lot more complicated, and harder to conclude successfully for many people.

But it's worth every second, and every penny. A rigorous hiring process is nothing compared to the problems you face when you have an unstable, unproductive or dysfunctional workforce. This approach to recruiting has improved the performance of our workforce so dramatically, it's not even a small question that both the cost and the effort are well worth it.

Onboarding and engagement.

Maybe you ran cross country in high school, or maybe you simply decided to take up running. Let's say you wanted to be able to do a five-mile run. That's a good goal, but if you've never run before, you wouldn't go out there and try to run five miles your first time out.

You'd never make it. You have to get yourself conditioned for a physical challenge like that, which means you start out with shorter distances and work gradually up to the level of performance you want to achieve.

That's just common sense when it comes to running, but most businesses don't apply the same common sense when it comes to starting a new employee.

We do. When we decide an applicant is a good candidate for a job, we explain that their first week will consist of half-days. (And yes, they're hourly, so they only get paid for half days. We explain that very clearly.) This not only minimizes our investment in new people who can't be expected to contribute much right away, but it also takes the pressure off them to do too much too soon.

That week of half-days is mainly spent shadowing another, more experienced employee. They're in a good position to learn, ask questions and observe how things work. It's also a chance to develop their physical conditioning. If the job is performed standing, and they're not used to standing for eight hours, that first week of half-days is like those shorter runs you do as you build up to five miles. It helps to get them ready for what will be asked of them all day, every day.

This approach yields us good results, but it also produces the occasional result that might surprise you. Many people do us a favor by quitting during their week of half-days. And I suspect they don't tell us the real reason.

It could be something as simple as the way another person looked at them when they made a mistake, or failed to grasp something. Not that we encourage people to be difficult or impatient with their colleagues – we don't – but the work environment is what it is, and you will sometimes experience that sort of thing. If it upsets you so much that you feel the need to quit during your onboarding period, then I don't think you would have lasted long at any rate.

Better that we find out now.

In the early going, we pay close attention to whether a new employee is really becoming engaged as part of our company. One test is how they would answer the question if another person asks about their job:

"Where do you work?"

"Grobbel's."

"What do they do?"

"They make corned beef."

That person isn't fully engaged with us. How do I know? Because a fully engaged person would say, "We make corned beef."

In the 2004 film "Miracle," which was about the 1980 U.S. Olympic hockey team, there's a scene that depicts the players in practice as being forced to skate suicides over and over. After each suicide, they were asked the question, "What's your name and who do you play for?"

Repeatedly the players would give their names and then identify their college team. They would have to skate the suicides again.

Finally one of them got it, gave his name and said, "I play for Team USA."

He finally engaged with his team.

It seemed harsh at the time, and some might read this today and think it doesn't matter. Who cares how he answers that question, one could argue, as long as he does his job well?

But when you look back to that 1980 U.S. Olympic hockey team, you'll recall that they won a game over a Soviet team that was thought to be vastly superior to them in terms of raw talent. How did they do that? Do you seriously mean to tell me it had nothing to do with heart, or with commitment, or with a belief in the nation and the flag they represented?

And do you seriously believe that a whole team sharing that commitment didn't represent an advantage over a nominally better team?

I mentioned earlier that we go through 30,000 applicants a year to pick out a few hundred we'll hire. Out of those, about 50 percent truly become engaged with our company. And that's a very good percentage. Getting to that 50 percent has improved our performance tremendously. But the other 50 percent tend to flame out in fairly short order, and we have to go through the process once again of replacing them.

It may seem time-consuming and expensive, but it's the only way to develop a high-performing team.

Supervision and leadership.

In January 2015, Ohio State won the first-ever college football championship that was decided on the field (not via polls as in previous years) in a championship playoff game. And I believe they had an unfair advantage, which might surprise anyone who remembers that they had to play the game with their third-string quarterback.

But they did.

Ohio State's head coach is Urban Meyer, and he's a master of the technical side of football. He also saw the need for leadership coaching, particularly since the program had been beset by scandal when he took it over three years earlier. So, Meyer sought the help of executive coach Tim Kight, who helped Meyer and the rest of his coaching staff develop the leadership side of the equation to go with the strategic acumen they already had.

The result?

A national championship.

Most organizations take people who are proficient at the technical side of the job and ask them to be supervisors. That's not entirely fair to them. The people side of the equation represents an entirely different set of skills and knowledge. Someone to supervise the technical aspect of the work is vitally important, and you should have a manager who knows how to do that extremely well.

But when issues arise with or among people, that requires a different kind of leader. We employ a personnel leader who works in concert with the technical supervisor.

Needless to say, it's essential that these two leaders work well with each other – that they respect each other's boundaries and areas of responsibility. Of course, that's part of our corporate culture as well. Members of the leadership team need to recognize that the team part is essential, and supporting the success of their colleagues is every bit as much a part of their jobs as succeeding in their own positions.

Once a supervisor understands the thinking behind this leadership model, he or she will almost always embrace it. And why not? You're more likely to succeed in your job if you're able to focus on what you do well, and if there's another person to support you in the areas that don't come as naturally to you.

And of course, it has to come from the top of the organization that these are company priorities. If that's communicated and practiced on a consistent basis, others on the leadership team will get the message and act accordingly.

Evaluation and Guidance.

It's the personnel leader who works with our people on their ACE skills – attitude, competence and energy.

That includes both proactive and responsive leadership. Every employee meets with the personnel leader, commonly called a check-in, for a 20-minute session once a month, just to make sure we're listening and understanding how people are doing. If there's an issue that needs to be addressed, this is when we have a regular opportunity to do it – which is not to say an employee can't raise a concern at any time. They can.

But the check-in sessions are very helpful and productive. The right personnel leader understands how to listen, and how to make sure the employee knows that we care about him or her on a personal level. Nothing is more important for a leader to do if he or she hopes to see employees give their best on a consistent basis. Employees will always do that for a leader that they know cares about them. When a leader doesn't care – or shows no signs of caring – some will still give their best because that's how they're wired. The entire workforce will not do so consistently.

Our personnel leaders update employees' ACE scores weekly. They get an A, B, C or D just like students in a school would get. This is all transparent and accessible to everyone online. And when a problem arises with an employee, the personnel leader addresses the issue proactively.

If their scores are low, we want to find out what's going

on with them. The personnel leader schedules a meeting as quickly as possible and takes a constructive, supportive approach. The idea is to identify and understand what might be causing the issue, and to work together with the employee to address it.

You don't know until you endeavor to find out. If the competence score is suffering because the employee is struggling with a particular, technical aspect of the job, you deal with that in one way. If the energy score is low because of a different kind of struggle – whether it's health, lack of sleep or something else entirely – that requires another approach.

And if the employee is coming to work every day with a terrible attitude, there's always something behind that. Once they're willing to admit the attitude issue, and they trust we want to help them and not scold them, they will usually be upfront about what's going on and how we can help.

I can understand why some people might resist the idea that we constantly monitor their scores, but there's a reason for it, and it's for their benefit. Situations can devolve into many issues quickly, and if something festers for several weeks without our knowing about it, we can find ourselves with a much more complicated problem to solve. An employee attitude issue, if left unaddressed for several weeks, can expand to include a lot more people and situations. When you can intervene quickly, you can usually deal with it before it has a chance to turn into something bigger and harder to manage.

That's what weekly monitoring of the scores allows us

to do.

Does it always work? No. No process is 100 percent foolproof. Sometimes the employee is either delusional or in denial, and absolutely can't see that there's a serious attitude issue – even though everyone else can see it.

But those situations are the exceptions. Usually the proactive approach yields excellent results, and we are able to deal with problems while they're still small.

This is why the guidance side of the equation is so important. The successful employee wants to understand what the supervisor needs and expects in order to achieve success, and helping them to get there requires good guidance that can help them understand – particularly if there's a problem to be addressed.

We believe that if an employee is struggling with a flaw or an issue, but wants to improve, we should provide all the support and guidance the solution requires. When employees refuse to acknowledge the issue, that's another matter and sometimes it doesn't end well. But most want to succeed, and this leadership model gives them the best opportunity to do so.

Process evolution and task fragmentation.

Here is where we truly channel our inner Henry Ford.

I talked in the earlier chapters of this book about how we changed our production process so we could more quickly train people to become productive contributors. That meant we could no longer expect every worker to master a complex, multi-faceted set of tasks. We had to replace more than

50 people in a matter of weeks, and it would have taken us months to train the new people to do things the old, complicated way.

So we took a completely fresh look at our process.

We broke the job of meat cutting down to eight separate steps, and asked each new employee to master only one of those steps. This simplified the training process tremendously, and made it possible for each person to become proficient, and then productive, within less than three weeks.

I realize that this change was born more from necessity than from brilliance, but our knowledge of Henry Ford's assembly line innovations gave us plenty of reason to think it could work. In fact, this change born of necessity has shown us a great deal about how to position employees to succeed in today's workforce.

As they master the fragmented tasks assigned to them, they not only grow in their productivity, they also have the opportunity to emerge as leaders for other members of the workforce.

And no one is suggesting that people must perform one task, and only one task, for their entire careers. The most valuable people are the ones who can learn to do many things. We should be careful not to force people into roles for which they're not suited – that whole square-peg-in-the-round-hole problem – but obviously an intelligent and skilled person has the ability to learn more than one simple task.

As opportunities present themselves, we give our people the chance to learn new tasks even as they continue to focus on the one, fragmented task to which they're assigned at present. That presents them with a variety of different opportunities. It might allow them to change assignments at some point in the future. Or as they learn more about the company's overall operations, it might position them for some sort of supervisor position.

But in the meantime, it's to their benefit that they have the opportunity to master a task and make it their own.

I was asked once if I think it demeans people to have them focus on just one task. I wonder if the guy who changes the tires in the pits at Indianapolis Motor Speedway feels demeaned because he does the same job all the time. I wonder if Tom Brady feels demeaned because Bill Belichick keeps telling him to go play quarterback.

I'm not trying to suggest that every task is necessarily the equal of every other task. But what workers are really looking for is the opportunity to be part of a successful organization that's doing things well and can provide opportunities both today and tomorrow. If we made everyone's job more complex and challenging, and the result was that we failed at our core mission, that wouldn't make the employees happier or more fulfilled. It would make them unemployed.

I've already established my belief that there is the perfect job for everyone. For most people, performing one-eighth of the task of trimming meat is probably not that perfect job. But if it puts you in a position to learn, and grow, and move toward that perfect job, then it's a good job for you to be in today.

The worst thing we could do to a good worker and good person is to ask more of them than our training or our system can allow them to succeed in. It makes more sense to position them, at every stage in the process, for success. As they grow in their skills and their knowledge, and they're ready to try to advance and learn more, we are happy to give them that chance.

One of the ways we do that is something we call Task Force Friday. I'd love to take credit for this idea but it actually came from one of our team members. Here's how it works:

We run full production only Monday through Thursday. By the end of the day on Thursday, our employees have gotten in their 40 hours. On Friday, they have the option of coming in to perform special tasks – everything from cleaning a piece of equipment to painting walls to grouting floors.

This is a meat processing facility. There is always a lot that needs to be done. And those who choose to participate in Task Force Friday get an opportunity to learn new tasks and new functions entirely apart from the one they perform on the other days of the week.

This is part of how we allow them to master one specific task while still learning and growing.

Those are the five pillars of ACE. It's how we take this ideal and turn it into reality within our workforce on a day-to-day basis.

Each of the five requires some serious investment. Each has challenged us to accept real change. There will always be some resistance to that, often starting at the top, where it can be hard for the boss to accept that there was anything about the old process that needed improvement.

Get past that. Please. This is a great process. It's rewarded us financially. It's also rewarded us by creating a work environment in which everyone really wants to work – and finds the experience of doing so fulfilling. That applies to everyone.

Including the boss.

9

The Culture of Respect:
Without It, Nothing Else Matters

The last two chapters spelled out a very ambitious program for how to build a workforce that is productive, fulfilled and committed to the objectives of your company. In Chapter 7, we explained the importance of attitude, competence and energy. In Chapter 8, we looked at the five pillars of a companywide approach to making it happen.

You're almost there.

But before you try any of this, you need to understand something: A company without a culture of respect will struggle to get the results it's looking for. And building a culture of respect – while arguably simple – is not easy. And it's not simply a matter of implementing certain policies and then sitting back to let them work.

A culture of respect is, above all else, about the values of leadership and how they are lived and practiced every day in the work place.

You might compare it to an unborn child. Once the baby has reached a certain point of gestation, he or she has the main elements required to sustain life. A beating heart. A functioning brain. Flowing blood. A digestive system. But with all that, the child can't survive unless surrounded by amniotic fluid. That's the necessary environment for life during this stage.

A corporate culture of respect is like the amniotic fluid that's necessary to make ACE work, and for the five pillars to be effective. Without it, you can do them all correctly but it won't make a bit of difference.

So how do you build a culture of respect?

For starters, the person at the top has to believe it. Not just as a business strategy. If it's insincere, people will sniff that out easily and it will fail. You must, as an employer, truly care about the people who work for you.

That does not mean you compromise on what's expected of them. Not at all. The company's success depends on their ability to produce at a high level, and their job security depends on the company's success. Very productive people are always better off than unproductive people, so if you care about them, your expectations of them should be high. The goals you set for them should be challenging.

And along with that, you should be putting them in a position to succeed in every conceivable way. You should be providing them with a work environment that fosters success and helps them when they are struggling. You should have clear and uncompromising standards, but you should also be patient and even generous in your support of people who want to achieve those goals and need help doing so.

The leader has to set the tone by letting other management-level people know two things unambiguously: 1. We care about every member of the team. 2. We will have no tolerance here for disrespect.

Now, how does that look in practice?

It starts with the language you use, and how you apply it in given situations. For instance, how do you deal with an employee who has attendance issues? Is your approach fact-based or judgment-based? It may seem like a small thing, and it's definitely subtle. But it makes a bigger difference than you realize.

If we tell an employee, "Your attendance is poor," we have done a lot more than simply define an issue to be addressed. We've essentially leveled an accusation and pronounced judgment. Now, you might ask, what's the difference? If the employee's attendance is significantly below what's expected, that's poor. Why not just say so and get it out in the open?

The reason is it's not necessary to add the element of judgment, and to put the employee on the defensive, in order to solve the problem. And in a culture of respect, solving the problem should be the goal, not the shaming of the employee.

"The required standard calls for you to miss no more than three days during the period we're looking at here, Jim. You missed 15 days. How can we help you to address this issue so you're consistently meeting the standard? What do we need to understand so we can help you?"

The facts are the same whether you use judgmental language or not. Jim won't be under the impression he's got a good attendance record because you declined to call it "poor" or "abysmal" or whatever other word you might choose. He gets it. He missed too many days.

So by taking a neutral, fact-based approach to the situation, we can encourage Jim to work with us in developing a solution to the problem. That's not going to work very well when you yell at him or otherwise denigrate him for his poor attendance record. You may think he deserves that, but even if you could defend that belief, you have to consider how it will play out in practice. Jim doesn't want you to believe he's a bad employee, so if you make that the issue, his understandable instinct is going to be to defend himself.

Now you're not talking about how to solve the problem. You're debating Jim's worth or lack thereof. That's not what you want to be talking about.

By dealing strictly with the facts and stressing the desire to work with Jim to make things better, you have a much better chance of getting Jim to partner with you in finding that solution. He's much more likely to be honest about the factors that are causing him to miss so many days, whether these are habits he needs to improve or issues in his personal life that he needs to deal with.

In all this, the message has to be consistent and clear that attendance meeting the standard is the only acceptable outcome. Jim needs to know that. This is not about establishing a standard for him that's different than everyone else's.

But Jim should also understand that he is valued and that the goal of the company is to help him meet the standard, so he can not only stay, but thrive.

If he can't meet the standard, he can't continue to work here. That doesn't mean he can't work anywhere. Not every job is as dependent as one of ours on consistent attendance. There are day laborer positions that allow you to work when you can show up, and don't consider it a problem when you can't. An employee who simply can't be consistent about showing up should look for work like that, because it's consistent with my belief that there is the perfect job for everyone. And if you're not in that perfect job, we may not be doing you a favor by bending over backwards to keep you.

Now let's consider a more extreme example: Let's say an employee is caught streaking naked through the plant. In this case, there is going to be no process seeking to solve the problem. The employee is going to be fired, plain and simple.

So in this case, you dispense with the neutrality and let them have it, right?

No. You don't. Not in a culture of respect. It probably sounds silly, but you're better off saying something like this:

"I really appreciate your enthusiasm, but the U.S. Department of Agriculture simply has not approved clothing-optional meat processing. So, while everyone here is going to miss you, we encourage you to find a clothing-optional workplace that will let you express your passion for that."

I realize I did not just tell the employee that his or her behavior was completely unacceptable. I don't need to do that. The outcome of the matter speaks for itself, but the point of my action is not to personally approve or disapprove. It's simply to follow policy and do what needs to be done for both the employee and the company.

What if the incident really makes me mad? That's irrelevant. What you feel has to be separated from the way you do your job. I realize that is hard for some people but they must learn how to do it. Whether that means taking a deep breath, or counting to 10, or whatever it is, you simply cannot allow your anger to manifest in the way you deal with employees.

Once it does, the culture of respect is compromised. And

you can't have that because a consistent culture of respect is transferred to the shop floor and every other aspect of the business. That's what I mean when I talk about refusing to tolerate disrespect. When a company's culture is built on respectful and courteous language, people get used to the idea that this is how they conduct themselves in a professional setting. The workers will get to the point where they set the example for newer colleagues.

If you join the company and you handle yourself in a disrespectful manner, you'll quickly find out this will not bring rewards. You adjust, or you won't last long. A company with a culture of respect will reject a person who refuses to be respectful – not by responding in kind but by making it clear that the disrespectful colleague can't join the company's mainstream while behaving disrespectfully.

If you're starting to see the value of achieving this, good. I thought you would. When you really think about what it means to have a culture like this, why wouldn't you want it? It not only makes for a much more pleasant environment but it prevents all kinds of problems that cost you time, money and productivity.

But I'm not going to mislead you: This is rarely executed successfully in the corporate environment. That's not because it can't be done. It's because companies aren't really prepared for what it will take to accomplish it.

One of the hardest steps is to make sure you have a management team that embraces this principle completely. That means successfully selling your existing people on it. It also means, from that point forward, making sure any new management hires are the kinds of people who will find this to be a natural and comfortable approach to take in the job.

The latter is actually easier. By using DISC profiles and other measurement tools, we can get a pretty good idea of the people who will embrace a culture of respect and operate consistent with it. If someone doesn't fit that profile, they might be a talented manager, but they're not for us. I'm sure there are companies who want the stern taskmaster who occasionally lets loose with a tirade. When I think we've got a candidate like that, I wish him well.

But I don't hire him.

It's harder to convince long-time managers, many of whom have built their careers operating in a different manner, that this is how it's going to be from now on. They may think you're questioning them and their techniques. They may doubt their own ability to be successful if they always have to operate in what might be a new and unfamiliar manner.

But it can be done. As always, it starts at the top. You must make them understand that you are personally committed to this, and even more so, that you personally believe in it. You have to make the case that it's not only in your heart, but that it's the right direction for the company.

That last point is the key, because it will be natural for many managers to assume a "culture of respect" means going soft, or lowering standards, or letting people off the hook when they do something wrong. You should make it clear that standards aren't changing, and that what was unacceptable yesterday is still unacceptable today.

What's changed is the way it's dealt with.

Let's go back to our employee who had the attendance issues. The manager who resists the culture of respect may well argue: "You're sugarcoating it. When they were hired, they agreed to be here every single day. They aren't living up to that. They need a kick in the ass because they made a commitment and they broke it."

The problem with this manager's position is that he's conflating the tone of the message with the strength and effectiveness of it. In the culture of respect, the facts, the standards and the potential consequences speak for themselves. The offer to help, which comes without the kick in the ass this guy wants to apply, is the only thing that can really solve the problem because it has the best chance of getting the employee's cooperation.

What this manager is really doing is venting his frustration. He's also projecting a bit, since he seems to think the employee will neither listen nor take the situation seriously if voices aren't raised and threats aren't issued.

In practice, this never improves employee receptiveness to an issue. Quite the contrary, it makes them feel under attack, and in the long term makes them nervous about how they handle themselves in the workplace. You don't want mistakes, of course, but neither do you want employees who are overly cautious because they're scared to death of making a mistake. If you're going to get yelled at or called a failure because you messed up, you're going to be on edge and less effective.

We want employees who feel comfortable and confident that they can do the job they've been asked to do, and that the company has their backs – certainly when they do well, but also when they make a mistake. And when someone does make a mistake, I want them to feel completely comfortable approaching their supervisor and telling him or her about it so it can be dealt with quickly and effectively.

Under which kind of supervisor do you think that's more likely? The respectful one? Or the yeller?

You know the answer.

By the way, another massive benefit of a culture of respect is a much, much lower rate of workplace violence. You can work out the value of that, right? People don't come to blows in an instant. It's the product of a tense atmosphere, and widespread disrespect feeds that tension. A culture of respect doesn't give that tension the opportunity to take hold.

It's true that consistency is crucial here, but perfection is not necessary. We all make mistakes sometimes, but in a culture of respect, we deal with them quickly and people don't hold grudges. And it's easy to come back from a mistake in a culture that puts a premium on solving problems and moving back in a positive direction.

What you're trying to give people here is what they really want, and it's not too much for them to ask for. They just want to matter. They want to count to someone. They want to feel they have value, not only to themselves but to others. They want to feel like if they had a problem or an issue, someone would consider it worth the time and effort to help them deal with it, because they are worth it.

In a culture that affirms that value for every person, you're not only giving people what they want but you're encouraging them to give it to their colleagues as well. They will understand that there's value to doing that.

I've had to work at this. I had to train my mouth not to be sarcastic and biting with people. I could easily sit here and tell you, "I'm Jason, and I'm a recovering perfectionist." It would be true. I've had to learn how not to come down hard on everyone who was falling short of my exacting standards.

You learn this lesson when the biting, sarcastic approach doesn't yield you the results you're looking for. You can constantly blame the other people involved for failing to live up to what you expect. But when you consistently get the same negative results, no matter who you're dealing with, it's probably time for you to consider the possibility that it's not them.

It's you.

I've done some mentoring in inner-city high schools, and I've talked to young people there about anger. Understandably, many of them displayed a fair amount of it. Maybe you would too if you had experienced what some of them have been through.

But anger is really just a manifestation of fear – one that seeks to impose the fear back on the other party. You can see this in dogs who have been abused. They often become vicious, and it's usually because the dog is afraid he will come in for more abuse unless he makes everyone else afraid of him first.

This is a very common behavioral trait of animals in the wild, too. In that environment, those who are perceived as weak will be attacked. So animals who fear they will be perceived as weak mask that fear with anger. They try to act vicious and aggressive in the hope of scaring off potential attackers.

And as most of us know, you don't need physical actions or even words to make someone else afraid of you. The stare-down can chill. The evil eye can terrify. I once heard a bank teller say to a customer, "You look mean when you don't smile." The customer was taken aback at first. I don't think he intended to look mean. But nonverbal signals are very powerful – all the more so when they are intended.

("I guess I'd better try to smile all the time," he said. She shook her head: "Then you'd just look goofy." Poor guy can't win.)

I realize there's no way you could ever enforce this, but I've often thought there should be three different categories of assault – physical, verbal and expression. The angry, menacing look can hurt you just as badly as the punch in the face or the verbal tirade.

I don't think people realize the signals they're sending to other people with the looks on their faces, or the potential hurt they can impose. I asked the high school students I was mentoring to consider a scenario:

Let's say you see a guy walking down the street, and he's

got a look on his face like he's ready to kill someone. He's got a saunter that signals he's ready to explode. Everyone has seen something like this. They've seen the look.

Now, not that I would recommend actually trying it, but what might happen if you went up to that guy and gave him a hug, and said, "I know you're just afraid inside, but it's OK. Everything's going to be all right."

The students all laughed. They thought there was a pretty good chance it wouldn't end well, and I'm sure they were right about that. But it's true that this guy is afraid, and that's why he's giving off this kind of countenance.

So let's apply this to the workplace. You're a co-worker or a supervisor. You can see that someone is telegraphing a lot of rage and hurt to those around him. How do you approach the situation?

It's absolutely true that we cannot tolerate a negative attitude in the workplace, so that standard has to be re-asserted in the clearest of terms. But how do you do that? Do you go up to the guy and yell at him, telling him that he's creeping everyone out and he'd better quit being pissed off or else? Or do you sit him down, let him know that you can see he's upset about something, and let him know you want to support and help him if you possibly can?

Look, I get it, some people don't want help and they don't want to stop being angry. For some people, being angry is what gets them up in the morning and what motivates everything they do. You can't force a person like that to accept your help, and it might become necessary to part ways with him or her.

But that is not the majority of people. The majority of people who are worked up about something want to calm down. They just aren't sure how to do it. The majority of people who are having a bad day at work want the day to get better. What they need is the chance to take a breath in a supportive environment where someone is willing to listen and obviously cares.

A company that operates with a culture of respect can help that person, can talk them down off the ledge if necessary, and turn what could have been a bad day into a good one. A company like that can take a person who's struggling and hurting and help them heal the hurt and become a happy, content, fulfilled employee.

But you have to know how to do it, and one principle to get you started is that you don't respond to anger with anger, or to disrespect with more disrespect. Remember the example earlier in the book about the scene from "The Breakfast Club"? This is the one in which the principal keeps adding on more detentions every time Judd Nelson's character defies him. Not only was that unnecessary because he had already made his point and applied justice, but it fed an angry situation that needed to be diffused.

How you approach a person struggling with hurt and rage is crucial. How you look at that person may be the most important factor in determining whether you can be successful at diffusing the situation. Do your eyes communicate concern and understanding? Or do they communicate anger and wrath?

I realize this kind of culture is not for everyone. There are workplaces that celebrate boisterousness. I could be totally wrong because I'm not speaking from direct experience, but my impression is that shipyards and steel mills tend to be like this. If that's the case, then the person who can't embrace a culture of respect in a company like ours can always go find work in a place like that. There's a perfect job for everyone! It just might not be in the first place you look.

And the culture of respect has to also come with a clear understanding of outcomes it can produce. I read a fascinating account of a problem that occurred with Korean Airlines precisely because everyone was so respectful.

Korean culture holds elders in very high regard, and when an older pilot is paired with a younger co-pilot, the older pilot always flies the plane. So what's the problem with that? The problem is that the younger co-pilot is never permitted to give the older pilot any feedback whatsoever. It would be considered disrespectful.

Korean Airlines hired a pilot from American Airlines to spend some time observing its operations and to make recommendations on where they could improve. One of the first things the American pilot recommended was that the more junior pilots should be the ones flying the planes. That would allow the more senior pilots to provide plenty of advice and feedback without violating protocols of respect that were so important in Korean culture.

He didn't ask them to abandon their culture of respect.

That would have helped no one. Instead, he asked them to make an adjustment to their operational model that would allow the culture of respect to become more of an asset.

There is a line of thought in American culture – and I think it influences our corporate culture as well – that to treat another person with respect is to be a namby-pamby wimp. People think that in order to be firm, they have to manifest anger and aggression and show disrespect. This is too often learned from parents, who make anger and raised voices a component of their discipline. You remember that when dad was being firm with you, he was yelling at you and he sounded mad. That's what you think it means to be firm.

It's not. Another air travel example comes to mind that sadly had tragic consequences.

An airliner from South America was coming into New York and was running low on fuel. When the pilot radioed the tower, he found himself dealing with an air-traffic controller who had what you might describe as a New York-style demeanor. (I'll apologize here to all the meek, polite New Yorkers who obviously would never act like this.)

This guy wanted to show the pilot who was boss, and he told the pilot he wasn't prepared to approve him to land just yet. The pilot felt it would be disrespectful to talk back to the controller, and even though he was running out of fuel, he backed down and tried to circle the airport as best he could until he was cleared to land.

That was a fatal mistake. The plane crashed.

And it was entirely unnecessary. The pilot didn't have to

back down to show respect to the belligerent air-traffic controller. He could have been firm but respectful.

"Sir, I understand your position, but with all due respect I am running low on fuel and we will crash if we don't land immediately. Now I need you to clear a runway for me to land immediately. I thank you and eagerly await your instructions."

I think that would have gotten results. It wouldn't have required an angry tone or the slightest increase in volume. It would have only required firmness and clarity.

And you'll notice that the statement I just wrote didn't include a single negative or biting word. That is never necessary to get your point across. Nor is it constructive in any way.

When you're always uplifting and positive with your words, you will win the day. People will be drawn to you. They will find dealing with you to be a pleasant and affirming experience.

What we're doing is teaching an entire company full of people how to treat each other like this, and how to enjoy the benefits of doing so. It's counterintuitive to some people at first. And sure, some just can't bring themselves to do it.

But most can. Not only that, but most are very happy when they master it. Most find that giving and receiving respect is really what they've always wanted, and that being in an environment that offers that respect every single day puts them in their ideal job setting.

This is what makes ACE possible. This is what gives the

five pillars a real shot at success. Develop the culture of respect, and you'll be amazed how much easier the other steps
are.

And needless to say, the rewards will astonish you.

10

The Rewards
(Why It's All Worth It)

I want to offer a shout out here to Herman Cain, with whom I connected through my collaborator Dan Calabrese. He wrote a book called The Right Problems that drew on his business experience to look at a principle that also drives this book.

In his book, he explained that you can't necessarily solve every problem you have all at once, and that you shouldn't try. What you should do instead is identify the high-leverage solutions – the ones that can not only solve their own corresponding problems but also lead to the solution of other problems.

For example, when you achieve greater economic growth, you not only achieve more widespread prosperity but you also put yourself in a stronger position to deal with problems like mounting debt, high unemployment and consumer spending power. You could try to develop different strategies to deal with each of those problems, but since the underlying problem is growth, it makes sense to first attack growth.

That's what it means to be solving the right problems.

The whole point of this book is to assert that the disposition of America's workforce is the right problem for the business community to be working on. Successfully doing so solves a myriad of other problems along with the main problem we'll be attacking.

Let's look at an example – streetlights. If you're having a hard time seeing how strengthening the workforce helps with streetlights, I understand. But let's really take a look at it.

In the City of Detroit, where my company is located,

the economy has been dominated for many years by three companies – General Motors, Ford and Chrysler (now Fiat-Chrysler). That stands in contrast to the many other cities whose economies might be dominated by as many as 25 or 30 major companies. In Detroit, these three dominant companies are all in the same business and, for the most part, do no business with each other.

As they've pulled away from the central city, they caused population to follow, as there were few viable, major employers left to pick up the slack. As a result, there were few incentives for young, career-oriented people to live in the central city, which resulted in the population of the city proper dwindling from a height of more than 1.8 million in the 1950s to under 700,000 today.

The people who remained tended to have lower incomes, and be much less consistent participants (if they were participants at all) in the workforce. And yet as the city's population dwindled, its geographic size remained exactly the same at 138.75 square miles.

All that land needs lighting, and the resources to operate the lights require a sizeable tax base from which to draw. Here's where Detroit has found itself at a very significant disadvantage compared with the communities around it.

In Detroit today, there are five street poles for every taxpayer. Imagine that. If you're a person who lives in Detroit and pays taxes, you are personally responsible for funding the operation of five streetlights. Meanwhile, in the suburbs that surround Detroit, there are typically five taxpayers for every streetlight. So, when it comes to the funding of street-light operations, the burden put on each taxpayer in the city is greater than the burden on each taxpayer in the suburbs by a factor of 2,500 percent.

What's the solution to that? Money? Well sure, but you're not getting at the underlying problem if you don't go any further than that. There have already been state funds and donated money raised to restore the streetlights. That's fine on a one-time basis, but to operate those lights you still need to draw from your tax base – and you can't do that if you're asking every taxpayer to pay for five streetlights.

Getting people back into the workforce, and getting the workforce more productive as a whole, generates more wealth and creates a much healthier environment in which to allocate taxpayer funds to use in operating streetlights. Fixing the workforce doesn't just improve our profitability and enhance our employees' quality of life. It also makes it more viable that we can see our way around town.

Let's look at another example – substance abuse.

People are responsible for their own choices, so this is not about excusing anyone for bad behavior, but no one can deny the statistical correlation between poverty and sub-stance abuse. More people in poverty means more societal resources devoted to dealing with the consequences of sub-stance abuse – whether that means more police resources to deal with additional lawbreaking, or more money spent on treatment, or more hospital capacity taken up by people who overdosed, or got in accidents, or got in fights... when a sober person would have just gotten home safe and sound.

(By the way, substance abusers are more likely to crash into streetlight poles, too.)

Getting more people into the workforce, and making them part of a workforce that is more productive on a per-worker basis, will result statistically in fewer substance abusers. Also, because a more productive workforce creates more wealth, you'll not only save the money you would have spent dealing with problems related to substance abuse, you'll also be creating even more wealth on top of that.

Imagine this: Everyone with more money. Much less money being spent dealing with substance abuse. And fewer people with personal problems in their lives caused by substance abuse.

You see how retooling the workforce is truly one of the high-leverage missions beckoning us to tackle it? And those were just two examples. I bet you could think of a whole lot more. Less money spent on public assistance programs. Lower tax rates, since you'd have more self-sufficient people to share the tax burden, and you could collect the same amount with lower rates on a per-person basis.

How about the vitality of the real estate market when there are more people with the capital to buy or rent high-value properties? How about the boost in consumer spending power that comes when worker incomes go up and productivity brings prices down? How about the potential to raise the personal savings rate and reduce personal debt, since that increased spending power gives you more cash on hand to buy what you need (or want) and leaves you less tempted to put it on a credit card?

These are just a few of the reasons this endeavor is so worth doing. Yes, it makes us better off. Yes, it makes our employees better off. But it also lessens or eliminates a whole host of other societal problems that demand our time, attention and resources.

And it all comes down to reinventing the way we do work, and the way we engage people at work. That invites people, particularly in our major cities, to not only rejoin the workforce but also to rethink the role it plays in their lives.

This is more than just a win-win. This is so many wins strung together, I'm tempted to say, "You'll get tired of all the winning." But I think someone else used that line already.

And I haven't even touched on the value you bring to the life of an individual when you give them the opportunity to experience the dignity of work.

I don't care what it is you do – it will touch your life in a positive way if you understand you are part of something worthwhile. You know what it feels like when you're lacking that, when you're not doing something you feel good about doing, or you're not part of a team that cares about you and values your contribution.

So it's not hard to understand how it blesses your life when these things become reality for you. And it doesn't even have that much to do with the actual task you're performing. It has more to do with knowing you're part of something worthy.

Consider the guy who works for a window-washing company, and whose job it is to replace the rubber strips on the squeegees. He's not the one washing the windows. He's not going up on the apparatus that takes him to the 27th floor. He just replaces the rubber strips on the squeegees. Pretty mundane, right?

Only if you treat it that way!

To the window-washing company that sees its work as an important mission, nothing is mundane. For the people in those buildings, the work this company does is the difference between seeing the world clearly every day and looking out through dirt and grime. If you've ever lived or worked in a building where you had to rely on someone else to clean the windows, you know exactly what I mean. If this happens too infrequently, it's the highlight of your month when the window washers finally show up, and everything is finally clear.

(If this isn't you, try letting your computer screen get filthy, and then go ahead and clean it. It's not all that different.)

The window-washing company that sees its mission in this way will have a much higher sense of purpose than one that thinks its job is merely mundane and ordinary. And when the mission really matters, then every part of it matters. There is every incentive for the rubber strip changer to master his or her craft – to get really good at it. And when you're a master of your craft at a company that really values its mission, you are going to be held in high esteem.

"But all I do is change the rubber strips on squeegees! It's not rocket science!"

Doesn't matter. What matters is that those people are looking out at a clear and striking view of the world, because of the great work your colleagues are doing with the squeegees that are performing at a high level of excellence. All because you're so good at changing those rubber strips.

By the way, speaking of rocket science, remember our discussion about how there's the perfect job for everyone? With all due respect to rocket scientists, we need them, but we don't need 300 million of them. Your perfect job is probably something else. And if you want to see a miserable rocket scientist, make him work all day long inside an office with grimy windows.

It takes leadership to make someone feel that their job has that kind of value. When the boss chooses to approach the company's function as a true and worthy mission, the employees are much more likely to follow suit.

That also works the other way around, unfortunately, and far too often given the current state of the workforce. Recent studies from major polling companies confirm that the number one reason people quit their jobs is neither money nor hours nor the nature of the work. It's the relationship with the boss. If it's not good – and too often it's not – people are far more likely to quit. And there is no reason that prompts them to quit more than this one.

Unfortunately, people are not as willing to admit that to those around them as they are to admit it to pollsters. You can imagine plenty of reasons this might be the case. If you say you're leaving for more money, it seems to reflect more positively on you because it appears you got a better opportunity. And if you don't much care for the boss, there's a pretty good chance you kept that to yourself during your time working for him. I suspect he knew it, but whether the issue was tension, hostility or lack of respect, these things are often understood but not said.

So what do you tell the boss when you quit? Well, you know, this new opportunity just seems to fit my goals and my needs at this time in my life.

It's a lot cleaner than telling him off, even though many are tempted and some give in to the temptation. The truth is we often keep our feelings to ourselves in the workplace because there's nothing to be gained by revealing them. But when we're asked in private by someone not connected to us, oh boy, we'll let loose then.

Bosses can do a lot to change this, and much of what we've discussed in this book can help make that happen. The culture of respect discussed in Chapter 9 leaves little room for tension and hostility, especially when bosses learn to avoid judgmental terms in meting out discipline or correction.

The right approach by bosses is crucial in establishing the dignity of work, which has everything to do with the satisfaction of work. Whatever you call it, it's crucial to the goal of bringing so many disaffected people back into the workforce.

Most people are going to be willing to do what gives them satisfaction. If it also earns them money and gives them a reliable way of supporting themselves and their lifestyle, so much the better. But not even money is a substitute for a rewarding, fulfilling purpose in life.

Every human being has a burning need to feel fulfilled, and work fills that need. The rush you get from a work achievement actually releases endorphins, in a way not all that different from what we experience during sex. (OK, it's different in some significant ways.) There's a reason we're drawn to experiences that give us a rush like that. And there's a reason we want to have those experiences again and again.

God is quite the genius, don't you think? He wanted us to procreate, so he connected that to an activity that gives us a rush we like, and want more of. He wants us to work too, and he gave us the capacity to get a similar rush from work. You get the same thing from working out. There's such a thing as a runner's high, which tends to occur when your body is working the hardest. It's an experience you can't get just sitting around.

I know people like their highs, and a lot of people have chosen chemicals as their means of getting them. That's too bad, because the highs you can get from perfectly natural and healthy things are better than any weed you can smoke or pill you can pop. If you're not getting those kinds of highs, you're missing out.

And sadly, far too many people are, especially when it comes to that high you get from work. They don't see the point in working to overcome the challenges they face in life. They've looked at what the workforce offers and they've determined – rightly or wrongly – that it just wasn't worth it for them to continue being part of it.

This is 40 percent of our able-bodied population. That's an astonishing number. It's bad enough when you consider how much productivity our economy is missing out on because these people aren't producing. But the far bigger tragedy in my mind is fulfillment and satisfaction that's missing from the lives of people who could be finding it in work.

I realize that some people who could be working make a perfectly rational choice to stay home with kids or attend to some other worthy priority. My point here is not that everyone who chooses not to join the workforce makes the wrong decision. I know that's not the case.

But we all know that far too much of that 40 percent of the population would be better off working, producing, earning a steady income and experiencing life as an accomplished, independent person. Most of the discussion in this book has been about economics and business – and rightly so because this is a business book – but how much would it impact our culture if such a large percentage of the population attained new levels of personal satisfaction in their lives? How would that affect societal attitudes? How would it impact what we expect from each other, from our employers, from government?

This needs to happen. And it can happen. And the business community doesn't have to go to Congress or petition the White House to do it. We can do it ourselves. We have the resources. We have the know-how. I've laid out the steps.

And I can already tell you it works because it's been working beautifully for my company.

Let's review them one more time:

ACE stands for Attitude, Competence and Energy. They're the three things we need most of all to instill and inspire in our people.

The five pillars of ACE are:

Recruitment and cultural fit
Onboarding and engagement
Supervision and leadership
Evaluation and guidance
Process evolution and fragmentation

When we put this system into place and saw how much it benefited us, my first instinct as a businessman was that I'd found myself quite a valuable trade secret. I should protect it and keep it as a competitive advantage.

But the more I thought about it, the more I realized that if I shared this with everyone, the societal benefits would be so great that my share of the benefits would more than make up for any competitive advantage I might theoretically be giving away.

Besides, it would help people, and that's always the right thing to do.

Business community, let's do this. Let's apply the steps laid out in this book and completely transform the American workforce, as well as the lives of everyone in it – and those who need to be back in it.

We don't need to ask permission. We just need to act.

Who's with me?

Acknowledgements

I want to thank the amazing team at Grobbel's, who were instrumental in the development of the ACE System. Laura Parvin, Kathryn McClelland, Dennis Lipps, Amber Mostiller, Allison Rosenberg, Russ Consiglio and Ryan Chapp. Also, my coaching and spiritual guide, Joe Grimm.

In addition, many thanks go to my editing team of Ryan Chapp, Justin Grobbel, and Emily Grobbel, along with the writing/editing team of Dan and Angie Calabrese.

And last but not least, the wonderful design and layout work of Samantha Grobbel.

I am truly blessed to have so many amazing people in the Grobbel's extended family!